BASIC

[BASIC]
Second Edition

Robert L. Albrecht

LeRoy Finkel

Jerald R. Brown

Dymax

John Wiley & Sons, Inc.

New York • Chichester • Brisbane • Toronto • Singapore

Library of Congress Cataloging in Publication Data

Albrecht, Robert L
  BASIC.

  (Wiley self-teaching guides)
  Includes index.
  1. Basic (Computer program language) - Programmed
instruction. I. Finkel, LeRoy, joint author.
II. Brown, Jerald, 1940-   , joint author.
III. Title.
QA 76.73.B3A4 1978 001.6'424 77-14998
ISBN 0-471-03500-9

Printed in the United States of America

    18 19 20 21

To the Reader

Tens of thousands of people of all ages have used the first edition of this book for a fast and thorough introduction to computer programming in BASIC. We have revised and updated this second edition to eliminate minor errors and typos, broaden the scope of the activities and examples, and provide some new material to clarify and extend your understanding of BASIC.

Since the appearance of BASIC, by Albrecht, Finkel and Brown, the field of computer science and the availability of computers to all people (non-professional computer users) has grown by leaps and bounds. Especially noteworthy is the appearance of the so-called personal or home computer. Integrated circuit technology has now provided us with computers far less expensive than ever before, yet with the same computing abilities as systems costing many times more. This means it will be easier for you, the beginner, the get "hands-on" computer programming practice in the BASIC language.

The development of the computer over the past two decades has been accompanied by much technical jargon and supposed complexity. We aim to clear away the mystery. With this book, you can teach yourself to control a computer. You will not only learn how to use the computer as a tool, but will also dispel forever the mystical aura surrounding the device. While there are certainly judgements to be made about *how* computers are used, the electronic hardware itself, like any tool, is neither good nor bad, and is not to be feared.

The computer language BASIC was developed at Dartmouth College by John Kemeny and Thomas Kurtz who recognized the need for an all purpose computer language that would be suitable for beginning programmers whose educational backgrounds would be varied and diverse. Beginners All-purpose Symbolic Instruction Code (BASIC) was originally designed as a simple language which could be learned in a few short hours. Over the years, improvements have been made in the language so that today, it may take a few days to learn the complete language but you will find you can do nearly anything you want in BASIC.

In this Self-Teaching Guide, you are learning the most widely used form of BASIC. It is very similar to Dartmouth BASIC, the common denominator of the versions of BASIC used by *many* computer manufacturers. Once you have mastered the basics of BASIC, you will find it quite easy to learn any variations or additional capabilities that may be available for the computer you use now and in the future. You should understand that not all BASICs are alike, though they are very similar.

An important feature of this book is the emphasis on reading and understanding a computer *program*, so that you can see why the program causes the computer to perform the task for which the program was written. You may have many occasions to *adapt* a program in BASIC written by someone else to your own needs. There is less and less need to write new programs that "reinvent the wheel". However, with the thorough grounding provided by this introduction to the BASIC language, and with the opportunity to practice and develop your skills, you will also be able to write programs for your own needs when no others are available.

This book is the result of the combined efforts of three authors with years of first hand experience in teaching college students and adults, and children to use computers and to program in BASIC. (We think you'll appreciate that as you successfully complete this book, especially if you have looked at other materials for learning BASIC.)

The prime purpose of the book is to teach BASIC. Of course, the application of the programming skills you learn will depend on your own interests. For this text, we have chosen a variety of examples ranging from the fields of social science, business, humanities to the simple statistics used in psychology, education and business. You do not need an extensive background in mathematics or science.

We hope you enjoy this easy, step-by-step method for learning BASIC.

RLA
LPF
JRB

Menlo Park, California
November, 1977

NOTE TO INSTRUCTORS: Based on feedback provided by users of the first edition of BASIC, we have included an extra self-test problem at the end of each chapter for which we do not provide a solution. You can use this "Bonus Problem" as an assignment for students to turn in as a group project or as an individual required assignment . . or any way you like. Remember, for most programming problems, many details and approaches in the solution of problems will differ from student to student. Yet, they may all still be correct in accomplishing the tasks set forth by the problem definition.

How to Use This Book

With the self-instructional format, you'll be actively involved in learning
BASIC. The material is presented in short numbered sections called
frames, each of which gives you a question or asks you to write a program.
Correct answers are given below the dashed line. For the best results, we urge
you to take pen or pencil in hand and to use a piece of thick paper or card-
board to keep the answers out of sight until you have written your answer in
the space provided. The questions are carefully designed to call your attention to important points in the examples and explanations, and to help you
learn to apply what is being explained or demonstrated.

At the end of each chapter is a Self-Test which provides an excellent
review of the material covered in the chapter. You may test yourself immediately after reading each chapter. Another good way of using the book is to
do a chapter, take a break, and save the Self-Test as a review before you begin
the next chapter.

Each chapter begins with a list of objectives — what you will be able to
do after completing that chapter. If you have had some previous experience
using BASIC and these objectives look familiar, you can use the Self-Test as
both a review and a guide showing where you should start following the text.
Try the Self-Test before reading the chapter. If you do well, study only the
frames indicated for the questions you missed. If you miss many questions,
start work at the beginning of that chapter.

At the end of the book is a Final Self-Test which will allow you to test
your understanding of BASIC.

This is a self-contained teaching program for learning the computer language called BASIC. However, what you learn will be theoretical until you
actually sit down at a computer terminal and apply your knowledge of the
computer language and programming techniques. We therefore strongly
recommend that you and this book get together with a computer. If you are
not enrolled in a course or employed in a business where computer terminals
are available, you can (with a little diligence) still get access to a computer
terminal. To practice using BASIC you have to have access to a system that
uses BASIC. Do some research on the availability of computer terminals
using BASIC in your community.

There are probably computer terminals in the high schools, community colleges and universities in your area. Be persistent, friendly and sincere until you find someone associated with the institution (faculty, graduate student, technician) who will allow you some "computer time" on a system using BASIC.

Some science museums and even a few libraries these days have computer terminals for public use.

Many businesses use computers. They may have their own "in-house" computer, or they may use a computer time sharing service.

You can rent a computer terminal to use in your home. You might get together with several friends to divide the cost. This is what is involved.

Computer terminal rental is about $65 a month, from a business that rents terminals (such as Western Union), computer time sharing companies and computer equipment companies. The terminal is equipped with a device that fits your regular home telephone.

Computer time sharing companies are located in most metropolitan areas. They are businesses that maintain computers that you "dial up" using a regular telephone. You establish an account with the company, and they issue you a telephone number and a code number, and then keep a record of the time that your terminal is connected to their computer system.

However, you must also pay the telephone bill if the time sharing company you use is a long distance or toll call. Hourly rates for "computer connect time" may run from $5 to $15 an hour, with rates as low as $2 per hour for evening or night use from some companies. Try the yellow pages of your phone book under "DATA PROCESSING" for time sharing services in your area.

BASIC will be easier and clearer if you have even occasional access to a teletype or other computer terminal so that you can try the examples and exercises, make your own modifications, and invent your own programs for your own purposes. However, computer access is *not* essential: all you need is this Self-Teaching Guide. You are now ready to teach yourself how to use BASIC.

Contents

CHAPTER ONE
Getting Started

When you complete this chapter, you will be able to:

- specify the correct format for entering a computer program (written in BASIC) into the computer;

- describe how to erase (SCRatch) an unwanted program from the computers memory, how to LIST a program currently in the computer, and how to RUN (process) a program;

- specify methods for correcting, editing, and deleting statements in a computer program;

- translate into everyday numbers the scientific or "E" notation used by computers for expressing extremely large numbers and extremely small decimal fractions;

- write programs to print information and do arithmetic, using PRINT statements and END statements and the correct BASIC notation for arithmetic operations.

1.   This first section starts off slowly and simply, to kind of ease you into things. There are several devices that are most commonly used for communication between a computer and the computer user.

Teletypewriter   CRT (Commodore Business Machines, Inc.)

What characteristics do these devices have in common?

  (a) television screen
  (b) a typewriter-like keyboard
  (c) a steering wheel

_____

  (b) a typewriter-like keyboard

2.   A computer *terminal* provides the means for communicating with the computer. By means of a teletype or other terminal, a computer program and data may be communicated to a computer. When the program is *run* or processed, the computer sends signals to the terminal which provides *output*— that is, the results of processing the program. Therefore, a terminal provides

_____ way communication between the computer and
      (one-two-)
the user.

_____

    two

3.   The *teletypewriter* is the most common device used for communication between the computer and its user, and it is the most common *computer terminal.* The teletype is used much as an electric typewriter. It prints the numerals 1, 2, 3, 4, 5, 6, 7, 8, 9, and 0; the letters of the alphabet; and some special symbols. Letters are printed in upper case (capitals) only. You may

not use the lower case letter L to stand for the numeral _____ .

_____ .

    one (1)

4.   So you want to know what computer programming is all about? Here's a computer program that will calculate a student's grade point average.

```
100 REMARK PRØGRAM TØ CØMPUTE GRADE PØINT AVERAGE
110 PRINT "HØW MANY UNITS ØF A";
120 INPUT A
130 PRINT "HØW MANY UNITS ØF B";
140 INPUT B
150 PRINT "HØW MANY UNITS ØF C";
160 INPUT C
170 PRINT "HØW MANY UNITS ØF D";        This is the program.
180 INPUT D
190 PRINT "HØW MANY UNITS ØF F";
200 INPUT F
210 LET U=A+B+C+D+F
220 LET G=(4*A+3*B+2*C+1*D)/U
230 PRINT
240 PRINT "YØUR GRADE PØINT AVERAGE IS";G
999 END

RUN

HØW MANY UNITS ØF A?4
HØW MANY UNITS ØF B?6
HØW MANY UNITS ØF C?6        This is the output or result
HØW MANY UNITS ØF D?0        of running the program above.
HØW MANY UNITS ØF F?0

YØUR GRADE PØINT AVERAGE IS 2.875
```

The program consists of 16 *statements*, each one on a separate line numbered 100 – 999. Each line begins with a line number. Following each line number is a statement that contains instructions to the computer.

This program was typed a line at a time on the teletype (or other terminal) and was saved in the computer's memory. Then we told the computer to RUN the program; that is, to follow the instructions in the program. During the run the computer, following the instructions in the program, asked for information (called input) to be supplied by the computer user – How many units of A's, B's, C's, etc., were received? The program then directed the computer to do the computation and print the result. By the end of Chapter Two, you will be able to understand and use all the BASIC notation used in this program and more, so read on.

The distinct lines in a computer *program* are called _____ .

––––––––––––––––––––––––––––

statements

5.   The computer stores a program in its "memory." Before the computer user attempts to enter a new program into the computer, he will want to remove any previous instructions that may be currently in the memory. To erase previous instructions in the computer, type the letters SCR, then press the key marked RETURN. SCR stands for SCRatch, and scratches out or

_____ any previous program in the computer.

––––––––––––––––––––––––––––

erases or removes

6.   Before a new program is typed into the computer, any old instructions held in the computer memory should be erased. To erase an old program,

type SCR and press the key marked _____ .

––––––––––––––––––––––––––––

RETURN

NOTE: Although most of the words and symbols in BASIC are the same for all computer systems that use BASIC, there are some exceptions. This is because there has not been a completely standardized form of the language that is used by all computer manufacturers. Common variations will be noted throughout this text. However, the concepts involved are the same, even though a particular code word or symbol may be different from that used here. When you have a grasp of BASIC, you will find it easy to make the substitutions necessary to use the particular computer system at hand, and a quick review of the BASIC reference manual for your system will provide you with any variations you need to know. For example, words such as NEW or CLEAR or START are used in place of SCRatch on some computer systems.

7.   Sample program:

```
1       LET A=5
10      LET B=10
135     LET C=A+B
277     PRINT A,B
852     PRINT C
9999    END
```

This program, written in BASIC, consists of six *statements*. Note that each statement begins with a *line number*.

From this example you can see that line numbers may range from _____ to _____.

_____

1 to 9999

(NOTE: the upper limit is different on some computers.)

8.   The line numbers indicate to the computer the order in which it is to follow the instructions in the program. It is not necessary for line numbers to follow each other successively (e.g., 1, 2, 3, 4, . . .) as you can see by looking at the line numbers in the program in the previous frame. However, it is more common to number by ten's as we have in the program below. Then, if we wish, more statements may be easily inserted in the program between existing statements.

```
10 LET A=5
20 LET B=10
30 LET C=A+B
40 PRINT A,B
50 PRINT C
99 END
```

This is a common way of numbering a program. Note that the line number for the END statement is 99. For convenience, we will use 99 or 999 or 9999 for the END statements, depending on the size of the other line numbers in the program.

How many new statements could be added between Lines 20 and 30? _____

––––––––––––––––––––––––––––

9 (Lines 21, 22, 23, 24, 25, 26, 27, 28, and 29)

9.   ```
10 PRINT 12 + 33
99 END
```

This is a very short program that is composed of only two statements.

Each statement begins with a line number. Circle the line number in each statement.

––––––––––––––––––––––––––––

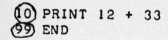
```
10 PRINT 12 + 33
99 END
```
```

10. **10 PRINT 12 ＋ 33**
    99 END

In this mini-program, Line 10 instructs the computer to evaluate the numerical expression 12 + 33, (i.e., do the arithmetic) and to PRINT the result. When this program is run on the computer, what will it print? _____.

_____

45 (the sum of 12 and 33)

11. The computer follows instructions in *line number order*. In the preceding program (frame 10) which statement is done first, Line 10 or Line 99?

_____.

_____

Line 10

12. **10 PRINT 12 ＋ 33**
    99 END

If you are seated at the computer terminal, and have erased any previous programs in the computer, you are ready to type in this program. To enter the program, type the first line, then press the RETURN key (RE-TURN) Then type the second line and _____.

_____

press the RETURN key

Note. By now, you should have determined whether to type SCRATCH, CLEAR, NEW or whatever is necessary to erase a program from the memory of *your* computer.

13. **10 PRINT 12 + 33**
     99 END

Assume you have typed this program into the computer. Now you wish the computer to process the program. Type RUN and press the RETURN key. If you have not made any typing errors in entering the program, the computer will evaluate 12 + 33, print the result 45, and stop. Here is what you would see on the teletype printout.

10 PRINT 12 + 33   The program you typed in.
99 END

RUN

45

Circle the command that tells the computer to begin to follow the instructions contained in the program.

_____

(RUN)

14. The program is not altered or erased from the computer's memory when you RUN it. Every time you type RUN and press RETURN the computer will RUN the program. Every time you RUN a program with the same information you will get _____ result.
                    (the same/ a different)

_____

the same
(An exception to this general rule will be discussed in Chapter Five.)

15. ```
10 PRINT "12 + 33"
99 END
```

Look at this program. How is it different from the previous one
(frame 13)? _____.

_____

The numerical expression is enclosed in quotation marks.

16. Note that the computer evaluated these two programs differently when
it was told to RUN them.

```
10 PRINT "12 + 33"      10 PRINT 12 + 33
99 END                  99 END
RUN                     RUN

12 + 33                 45
```

The statement

```
        PRINT 12 + 33        (Without " ")
```

tells the computer to evaluate the *numerical expression* 12 + 33 (i.e., do the
arithmetic) and print the result as a decimal numeral.

The statement

```
        PRINT "12 + 33"    (With " ")
```

tells the computer to print the *string* enclosed in quotation marks *exactly as
it appears*. No arithmetic is performed.
   In BASIC, a string is information in a PRINT statement that is enclosed

by _____.

_____

quotation marks
```

17. Fill in the blank as the computer would print it.

```
20 PRINT "186 - 58"
25 END
RUN
```

_____

----

186 − 58   (Note that the computer does not print the quotation marks.)

PRINT "MY HUMAN UNDERSTANDS ME"

18. The underlined portion of the statement is a string. It is enclosed in quotation marks.

PRINT "12 + 33"   **PRINT 12 + 33**

This is a string. It is enclosed   This is not a string. It is a
in quotation marks.   numerical expression.

A *string* may include

   (a) numerals (0, 1, 2, . . .)
   (b) letters (A, B, C, . . .)
   (c) special characters (+, −, *, /, ↑, comma, period, semicolon, etc.)

Since quotation marks define the beginning and end of a string, they

_____ be used as a character in the string.
   (can/cannot)

----

cannot

19. If you wish to change one or more statements in a program currently in the computer, you may do so *without* SCRatching the program and starting over. You merely type in a new statement, using the *same line number* as the line you wish to replace. Look at the program below, and the change made in it by replacing one line.

```
SCR
                    SCRatch the preceding program.

10 PRINT 7 + 5
99 END              Enter the new program.

RUN                 RUN the new program.

12                  Here is the result.
```

Next . . . *replace* Line 10 with a new Line 10. (*Replace* means retype the line, beginning with the line number.)

```
10 PRINT 6*9
```

Now tell the computer to LIST the current program. To do this, you type LIST and press the RETURN key.

```
LIST

10 PRINT 6*9 ◄─ Here is the new line 10,
99 END   ◄──────── and the old Line 99.

RUN              RUN the modified program.

54               Here is the new result.
```

You may change or replace any line in your program by retyping it, using the same line number as the line you wish changed. The new statement

_____the old one with the same line number.

_____

replaces (or changes)

Remember. To tell the computer to type a copy of the current program, type LIST and press the RETURN key.

20. While we're on the subject, suppose you wish to take a statement out of a program *without* replacing it with another statement. *Don't* SCRatch and start over. Merely type the line number of the statement you wish deleted or removed and press RETURN.

```
10 PRINT 5+5     This program is in the computer,
20 PRINT 12+3  ← and we wish to delete (remove)
30 PRINT 6+4   ← Lines 20 and 30.
99 END
```

```
20          ←————— Type the line numbers only, and
30          ←————— press RETURN after each.
```

```
LIST            Now, LIST the program.

10 PRINT 5+5
99 END          Presto! Lines 20 and 30 are gone.
```

Here is another program and a RUN of the program:

```
10 PRINT "MY COMPUTER UNDERSTANDS ME"
20 PRINT "MY COMPUTER CONFUSES ME"
99 END

RUN

MY COMPUTER UNDERSTANDS ME
MY COMPUTER CONFUSES ME ←
```

This offends us, so we want to delete the statement in the program that caused the computer to print it, and we want a RUN of the program to look like this:

```
RUN

MY COMPUTER UNDERSTANDS ME
```

(a) What would you do to remove the offending statement from the program? _____.

(b) Show a LISTing of the program with the offending statement removed:

_____

(a) Type 20 and press RETURN

(b) **LIST**

   10 PRINT "MY CØMPUTER UNDERSTANDS ME"
   99 END

NOTE: The quotation marks are included because this is a LISTing of the program itself, and not a RUN of the program.

Summary of operations:

SCR, NEW or CLEAR — erases the current program

RUN — executes the current program

LIST — prints a list of the current program

Line number, RETURN — deletes the statement with line number indicated

21. When typing your programs into the computer, you may make a typing error or some other mistake. Look at this example.

10 PTINT 2∗3+4   We misspell PRINT.

SYNTAX ERRØR   The computer tells us we made a mistake.
(Some computer systems do not inform you
of errors until you try to RUN the program.)

The error message may be different on your computer. That's not the point.
The point is, if you had noticed that you hit T when you meant to hit R,
you could have immediately corrected your mistake by using the *back
arrow* (←).

**BEWARE! This method for correcting mistakes may not
work on your computer. If it doesn't, ask someone how
to make corrections.**

The back arrow ← is on the same key as the letter O. To type a back arrow,
hold the SHIFT key down and press:

Here is an example of how to correct a typing error.

SCR

10 PT←RINT 2∗3+4   The back arrow (←) deletes the character that
99 END   it points to. Note: no space(s) after the back arrow.

LIST   LIST the program by typing the word LIST and
pressing RETURN.

10 PRINT 2∗3+4   The statement is O.K.
99 END

Now look at this example:

10 PRINT "MY HUMAN UNN←DERSTANS ←←DS ME"
99 END

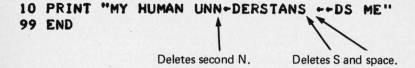

Deletes second N.   Deletes S and space.

Show how the computer would print a LISTing of this latest program.

LIST

10 PRINT "MY HUMAN UNDERSTANDS ME"
99 END

*Again, the quotation marks are included because this is merely a
LISTing of the program itself, not a RUN of the program.*

22. Assume you just sat down at the computer terminal. You wish to
know if there is a program currently in the computer's memory. Type LIST
and then press the RETURN key. The computer will automatically type
out the program (if there is one) that is in its memory. Here is an example.

LIST

10 PRINT "12 + 33"   The computer automatically typed all this.
99 END

Circle the command in the example above that caused the computer to type
out the program already stored in its memory.

----

23. **10 PRINT "12 + 33"**
    99 END

Assume that this program is currently in the computer's memory. Now you wish to add a new statement to the program, that says PRINT 12 + 33. You want the new statement to be evaluated by the computer *after* PRINT "12 + 33." The line number for the new statement must be greater than _____ and less than _____ .

_____

greater than *10* and less than *99*.

24. **10 PRINT "12 + 33"**
    99 END

This program is stored in the computer. We type in the following statement:

20 PRINT 12 + 33

and then press the RETURN key. The new statement is then incorporated into the existing program. To verify this, type LIST, then press the RETURN key. The computer will type out the program with the new statement in line-number order. Fill in the blanks to show what the computer will print.

LIST

_____

_____

_____

_____

_____

10 PRINT "12 + 33"
20 PRINT 12 + 33
99 END

25. If you type RUN with the preceding program in the computer, the computer would print:

```
RUN

12 + 33
 45
```

If you retype Line 10 and added a comma to the end of the statement, the program would look like this when LISTed:

```
LIST

10 PRINT "12 + 33",
20 PRINT 12 + 33
99 END

RUN

12 + 33          45
```
Note that the two results are printed on one line.

Here is a variation of the program that causes the computer to print the problem (i.e., the string enclosed by quotation marks) and the answer on the same line.

```
10 PRINT "12 + 33 =" , 12 + 33
99 END

RUN

12 + 33 =      45
```

Here is another program. Fill in the blank to show what the computer would print.

```
10 PRINT "TWELVE PLUS THIRTY THREE EQUALS" , 12 + 33
99 RUN

RUN
```

_____

- -

```
TWELVE PLUS THIRTY THREE EQUALS    45
```

26.   In BASIC, the comma and semicolon permit several expressions and/or strings to be printed on the same line. Look at the results of these two programs.

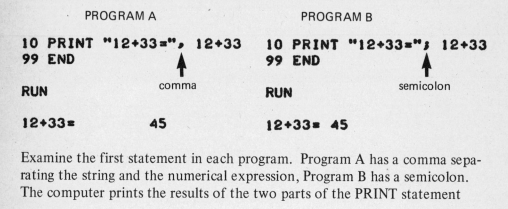

Examine the first statement in each program. Program A has a comma separating the string and the numerical expression, Program B has a semicolon. The computer prints the results of the two parts of the PRINT statement *closer together* if you use a _____ instead of a _____.

_____

semicolon instead of a comma

27.   On most computers using BASIC, there are 5 standard *print positions* across a teletypewriter line. A comma in a PRINT statement causes the teletypewriter to move to the next available print position. For example,

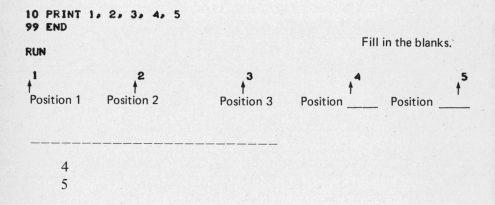

_____

4
5

NOTE: Some computer programs and RUNs have been reduced to save space.

28. Did you notice that the little arrows in the above example seem to be pointing to the space to the left of the number? This is where the print position actually begins. When the computer prints a positive number or zero, it prints a space first, then prints the digits of the number. Watch what happens when *negative* numbers are printed below positive numbers.

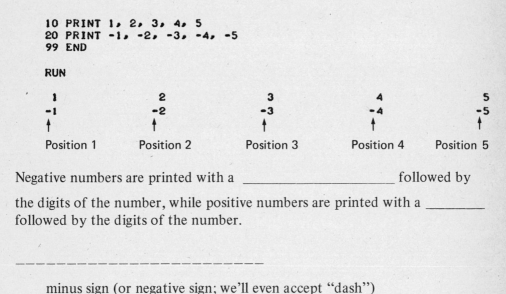

```
10 PRINT 1, 2, 3, 4, 5
20 PRINT -1, -2, -3, -4, -5
99 END

RUN
```

```
    1               2               3               4               5
   -1              -2              -3              -4              -5
    ↑               ↑               ↑               ↑               ↑
Position 1      Position 2      Position 3      Position 4      Position 5
```

Negative numbers are printed with a _____ followed by the digits of the number, while positive numbers are printed with a _____ followed by the digits of the number.

_____

minus sign (or negative sign; we'll even accept "dash")
space

29. But what happens if there are *more than* 5 things in a PRINT statement? Watch.

```
10 PRINT 1, 2, 3, 4, 5, 6, 7, 8
99 END

RUN
```

1	2	3	4	5
6	7	8		

The computer prints the 8 numbers on 2 lines with _____ numbers on the first line and _____ numbers on the second line.

_____

5
3

30. Got it? What will the computer print during the following RUN?

```
10 PRINT 1, 2, 3, 4, 5, 6, 7, 8, 9, 10, 11, 12
99 END

RUN
```

_____

1	2	3	4	5
6	7	8	9	10
11	12			

31. Now check what happens when we use *semicolons* instead of commas
to separate things in a PRINT statement.

```
10 PRINT 1; 2; 3; 4; 5
99 END

RUN

 1   2   3   4   5
```

```
10 PRINT 1; 2; 3; 4; 5; 6; 7; 8
99 END

RUN

 1   2   3   4   5   6   7   8
```

Semicolon spacing varies from computer to computer. The above RUNs
show how our computer does it. Things get printed closer together
when we use a _____ instead of a comma.

_____

    semicolon

With semicolon spacing, most versions of BASIC print positive numbers as
space, digits, space. Negative numbers are printed as minus sign, digits, space.
For example,

```
 1   12   123   1234   12345
-1  -12  -123  -1234  -12345
```

Trailing space printed *after* the digits of the number.

32. Now let's see what happens when commas are used to separate two or more strings in a PRINT statement.

```
10 PRINT "THIS","IS","COMPUTER","PROGRAMMING?"
99 END

RUN

THIS            IS              COMPUTER        PROGRAMMING?
↑               ↑               ↑               ↑
Position 1      Position 2      Position 3      Position 4
```

In this PRINT statement, there are 4 strings, separated by commas. Each string is printed in a standard printing position. Here is a similar program using semicolons instead of commas.

```
10 PRINT "THIS";"IS";"COMPUTER";"PROGRAMMING?"
99 END

RUN

THISISCOMPUTERPROGRAMMING?     ◄──────── No spaces are printed.
```

As you can see, with semicolon spacing,_____ spaces are printed between strings.

_____

no (or zero)

33. If you want spaces, include them in the strings.

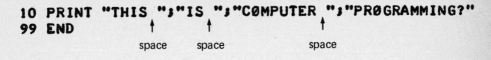

```
10 PRINT "THIS ";"IS ";"COMPUTER ";"PROGRAMMING?"
99 END
```
           ↑   ↑   ↑

     space   space   space

If we RUN this latest program, what will be printed?

_____

_____

THIS IS COMPUTER PROGRAMMING?

(Yes, this really is computer programming, although somewhat rudimentary. But read on!)

34. You have probably noticed that the plus (+) symbol of arithmetic tells the computer to add. The minus (−) symbol tells it to subtract. (It also indicates negative numbers.) The symbol for multiplication in BASIC is the asterisk (*), and the slash (/) is the symbol for division.

```
TØ TELL THE CØMPUTER TØ ADD, USE        +
TØ TELL THE CØMPUTER TØ SUBTRACT, USE   -
TØ TELL THE CØMPUTER TØ MULTIPLY, USE   *
TØ TELL THE CØMPUTER TØ DIVIDE, USE     /
```

Remember, when you want the computer to squeeze the answers or output more closely together, use semicolons instead of commas in the PRINT statement.

Here is a sample program to do simple arithmetic, with the results of a RUN of the program. Note the use of commas, and the widely spaced answers.

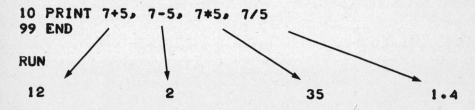

```
10 PRINT 7+5, 7-5, 7*5, 7/5
99 END

RUN

   12            2            35           1.4
```

Write a short program to do the following simple arithmetic. Group all of the expressions in one PRINT statement, using commas to separate expressions. Show the results you would predict for a RUN of your program, then try it on the computer if one is available.

10 + 6   15 − 9   23 ÷ 5   3 × 13

- -

```
10 PRINT 10+6, 15-9, 23/5, 3*13
99 END

RUN

   16            6            4.6          39
```

35. Here are some BASIC expressions in which two or more operations are used. For some of these expressions we have shown the value computed by the computer after it does the indicated arithmetic. You complete the rest.

Expression	Value Computed by Computer
2*3 − 4	2
2 + 3*4	14
2*3 + 4*5	_____
2 + 3*4 − 5	_____
2*3 − 4*5 + 6*7	_____

_____

26
9
28

36. Here are some more examples and exercises, using division (/).

Expression	Value Computed by Computer
3/4 + 5	5.75
2 − 3/4	1.25
2*3 + 4/5	6.8
3/4 + 5*6	_____
2 − 3/4 + 5	_____

_____

30.75
6.25

37.

> The computer does arithmetic in *left* to *right* order, with all multiplications (*) and/or divisions (/) performed *before* additions (+) and/or subtractions (−).
>
> $$\left.\begin{matrix} * \\ / \end{matrix}\right\} \text{ before } \left\{\begin{matrix} + \\ - \end{matrix}\right.$$

Now try these. *(REMEMBER: Do arithmetic in left to right order.)*

Expression	Value Computed by Computer
2*3/4	_____
3/4*5	_____
3/4/5	_____
2*3/4 + 3/4*5	_____

- -

1.5   Multiply 2 by 3, then divide result by 4.
3.75 Divide 3 by 4, then multiply result by 5.
.15   Divide 3 by 4, then divide result by 5.
5.25 First compute 2*3/4, then compute 3/4*5 then add the two
         results.

38. If you want to change the order, use parentheses.

2*3 + 4 = 10

but   2*(3 + 4) = 14   Compute 3 + 4, then multiply result by 2.

2 + 3*4 + 5 = 19

but   (2 + 3)*(4 + 5) = 45   Compute 2 + 3, then compute 4 + 5, then
                                                multiply those two results.

Complete the following. *(REMEMBER: Operations in parentheses are done first.)*

Expression	Value Computed by Computer
(2 + 3)/(4*5)	_____
2 + 3*(4 + 5)	_____
1/(3 + 5)	_____

.25
29
.125

39. One last look at the order in which arithmetic is done. In the expression below, the arrows in the circles show the order in which the operations are carried out. Write the final value for each expression.

Expression   Value Computed by Computer

⑤ ④ ③ ② ①
2 + 3 * (4 − (5 + 6 * 7))   _____

① ③ ② ④ ⑤
(3 * 4 + 5 * 6 − 7) / 8   _____

−127
4.375

40.   Your next task is to write a correct BASIC expression to solve a given problem. Do so for each of the following.

> Remember to indicate all multiplication and division operations with the proper BASIC symbol.

Problem	BASIC Expression
$2 \times 3 + 6 \div 7$	_____
$16(33 - 21)$	_____
$3.14 \times 2 \times 2$	_____
$\dfrac{88 - 52}{18 + 47}$	_____

2*3 + 6/7
16*(33 − 21)   (Did you forget the asterisk?)
3.14*2*2
(88 − 52)/(18 + 47)

41. Write a complete BASIC program to compute and print the values of the expressions in frame 40. A RUN of your program should produce the following results.

```
RUN

   6.85714
   192
   12.56
   .553846
```

```
10 PRINT 2*3+6/7
20 PRINT 16*(33-21)
30 PRINT 3.14*2*2
40 PRINT (88-52)/(18+47)
99 END
```

42.   There is a fifth arithmetic symbol in BASIC, which indicates raising a number to a power. This operation is called *exponentiation*.

   ↑ means raise to a power

For example,

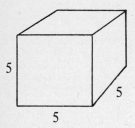

Volume of a cube: $V = S^3$, where S is the length of a side.

If $S = 5$ and $V = 5^3$, then

$V = 5^3 = 5 \times 5 \times 5 = 125$.

Since a teletypewriter cannot print superscripts, you tell the computer to raise a number to a power by using the symbol ↑ . On the teletypewriter, depress the SHIFT key and hold it while you press the ⟨↑ N⟩ key.

10 PRINT 5↑3   (5↑3 means 5^3 or 5 x 5 x 5)
99 END

RUN

   125

Now, fill in the RUN for this one.

10 PRINT 2↑6   (2↑6 means 2^6 or 2 x 2 x 2 x 2 x 2 x 2)
99 END

RUN

   _____

_ _

   64

43. Write a BASIC expression for each problem.

Problem   BASIC Expression

(a) $2^5 + 3^4$ _____

(b) $7 \times 7 \times 7 \times 7 \times 7 \times 7 \times 7$ _____

```
2↑5 + 3↑4
7*7*7*7*7*7*7  or  7↑7
```

44. When evaluating a mixed expression of arithmetic operations, the computer computes powers (↑) *before* doing multiplication, division, addition, or subtraction.

The formula for computing the area of a circle is

$$A = \pi r^2$$

Let's use 3.14 as an approximate value of π and write a program to compute the area of a circle of radius 7.

```
10 PRINT "IF RADIUS IS 7, AREA ØF CIRCLE IS"; 3.14*7↑2
99 END

RUN

IF RADIUS IS 7, AREA ØF CIRCLE IS 153.86
```

In computing 3.14*7↑2, the computer first computes _____ , then multiplies that result by _____ .

```
7↑2      (7↑2 = 7 × 7 = 49)
3.14
```

45. Computers use a special form of notation to indicate extremely large numbers, or extremely small decimal fractions. This method of expressing numbers is called *scientific notation*. Consider, for instance, a large number like the population of the earth which is about 4.1 billion people:

    4.1 billion = 4 100 000 000

We asked *our** computer to print the population of the earth:

```
10 PRINT 4100000000
99 END

RUN

   4.100000E+9          What's this?
```

Our computer printed the population of the earth in a form of *scientific notation*. (It really isn't especially scientific . . . it's just called that by some people.)

    Scientific notation is simply a shorthand way of expressing very large or very small numbers. In scientific notation a number is represented by a *mantissa* and an *exponent:*

        mantissa   exponent

The mantissa and the exponent are separated by the letter _____.

_____

    E

* Your computer may do it somewhat differently.

46. Here are some examples showing numbers written in good old every day notation and again in scientific notation (well, scientific notation according to our computer).

One trillion

    ordinary notation: 1 000 000 000 000
    scientific notation: **1.000000E+12**

Volume of the earth in bushels

    ordinary notation: 31 708 000 000 000 000 000 000
    scientific notation: **3.170800E+22**

Speed of a snail in miles per second

    ordinary notation: .0000079
    scientific notation: **7.9000000E-6**

In each number above expressed in scientific notation, underline the mantissa and circle the exponent.

––––––––––––––––––––––––––––

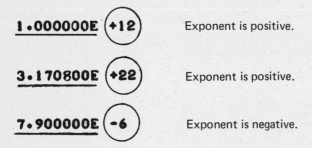

1.000000E (**+12**)   Exponent is positive.

3.170800E (**+22**)   Exponent is positive.

7.900000E (**-6**)   Exponent is negative.

Have you noticed? Our computer always prints the mantissa with 7 digits, one digit to the left of the point, 6 digits to the right.

47. Numbers printed in scientific notation can be converted to ordinary notation as follows.

CASE 1. Exponent is positive.

(1)   Write the mantissa separately.

(2)   Move the decimal point of the mantissa to the RIGHT the number of places specified by the exponent. If necessary, add zeros.

EXAMPLE: 6.123456E+4

(1) 6.123456   (2) 6. 1234.56

                     4 places

Therefore, 6.123456E+4 = 61234.56.

EXAMPLE: 3.600000E+9

(1) 3.600000   (2) 3. 600000000 .

                     9 places (we had to add zeros)

Therefore, 3.900000E+9 = 3900000000.

Now you try it: 1.234567E+13

(1) _____   (2) _____

Therefore, 1.234567E+13 = _____

1.234567
1.2345670000000.
     13 places (add 7 zeros)

12345670000000.

48. CASE 2.   Exponent is negative.

(1)   Write the mantissa separately.

(2)   Move the decimal point of the mantissa to the LEFT the number of places specified by the exponent. If necessary, add zeros.

EXAMPLE: 7.900000E−6

(1)   7.900000   (2)   .000007 . 900000

6 places (we added 5 zeros)

Therefore: 7.900000E−6 = .0000079

Your turn: 1.234567E−5

(1) _____   (2) _____

Therefore, 1.234567E−5 = _____

_____

1.234567
.00001 . 234567

5 places (we added 4 zeros)

.00001234567

SELF-TEST

If you can answer these questions, you are a budding computer user and are ready to go on to Chapter Two.

1.   The device used to communicate programs to a computer is called a

      _____ .

2.   The individual lines of computer instructions in a program are called

      _____ .

3.   What is missing from this short program?_____

```
PRINT 2+2
END
```

4.   Assume that you are at a computer terminal, typing a statement into the computer, and you notice that you have made a typing error. Describe a method of correcting your error (other than completely retyping the statement).

5.   Describe a method for replacing a new statement for an old statement in a program without erasing the entire program and starting over.

6.   Assume that there is a program in the computer. How do you erase that program from the computer's memory?

7.   Assume that there is a program in the computer. How do you tell the computer to actually follow (or process) the program?

8. How do you cause the computer to type out a program stored in its memory?

9. Assume that this program is in the computer.

```
10 PRINT 3*5
20 PRINT 8↑3
99 END
```

Describe how to delete (remove) the second statement without erasing the entire program.

10. Write the symbols used in BASIC for the following arithmetic operations.

addition   _____

subtraction   _____

multiplication   _____

division   _____

powers   _____

Refer to this program to answer questions 11 through 18.

```
10 PRINT "MY COMPUTER IS A WHIZ AT ARITHMETIC."
20 PRINT 5+2*4↑3
30 PRINT 8-16/32
40 PRINT (5+2)*(8-3)
50 PRINT "THAT'S ALL, FOLKS!"
99 END
```

11. Which statements contain strings? _____

12. A string begins and ends with _____.

13. Describe the order in which the computer does the arithmetic in Line 20.

14. Describe the order in which the computer does the arithmetic in Line 30.

15. Describe the order in which the computer does the arithmetic in Line 40.

16. In Line 40, why does the computer do the addition before the subtraction?

17. In general the computer does multiplication and division before addition and subtraction. Why is the order changed in Line 40?

18. Show what the computer will print when the program is RUN.

19. What symbol is used between several strings or expressions in a PRINT statement to cause the results to be printed close together when the program is RUN? _____

20. Look at this program.

```
10 PRINT 10,20,30,40,50,60,70
99 END
```

How many *lines* will the results of RUNing the program occupy? _____

21. Convert the following numbers from scientific or "E" notation into standard notation.

Scientific Notation	Ordinary Notation
1.123456E+6	_____
1.123456E+12	_____
7.777777E−2	_____
1.000000E−12	_____

BONUS PROBLEM. Write a computer program to do the following arithmetic and produce the results shown in the RUN below.

(a) 10^3

(b) 10^{12}

(c) $\dfrac{18.56 - 9.35}{2.12 + 3.33}$

RUN

```
TEN RAISED TØ THE 3RD PØWER = 1000
TEN RAISED TØ THE 12TH PØWER = 1.000000E+12
THE ANSWER TØ PRØBLEM (C) IS 1.689908
```

Answers to Self-Test

1. Computer terminal (e.g., teletypewriter). (frames 1 to 3)

2. Statements   (frames 4 to 7)

3. Line numbers (frames 7 to 9)

4. Type a back arrow (←) to erase each character (right to left) that you wish deleted until the mistake is erased. Then finish typing the statement, beginning at the point where the error was made. (frame 21)

5. Using the line number of the statement you wish replaced, type in the new statement. (frame 19)

6. Type SCR (for SCRatch), and press the RETURN key. (frames 5 & 6)

7. Type RUN and press the RETURN key. (frame 13)

8. Type LIST and press the RETURN key.   (frames 19 to 22)

9. Type the line number of the line to be deleted (20) and press the RETURN key. (frame 20)

10. +   addition
    −   subtraction
    *   multiplication
    /   division
    ↑   powers   (frame 34)

11. Lines 10 and 50. (frames 15 to 18)

12. Quotation marks   (frames 15 to 18)

13. ↑, *, +. First the computer computes $4 \uparrow 3$, multiplies the result by 2, then adds 5. (frames 35 to 37 and frame 44)

14. /, −. First the computer divides 16 by 32, then subtracts the result from 8. (frames 35 to 37)

15. +, −, *. First the computer adds 5 and 2, next it subtracts 3 from 8, and then it multiplies the two results. (frames 38 to 40)

16. The computer does the operations contained in parentheses in left to right order. (frames 38 to 40)

17. The computer does arithmetic contained in parentheses first. (frames 38 to 40)

18. **RUN**   (frames 38 to 40)

```
MY COMPUTER IS A WHIZ AT ARITHMETIC.
 133
 7.5
 35
THAT'S ALL, FOLKS!
```

19. Semicolon.   (frames 26 and 31)

20. Two lines, like this:

```
    10           20              30              40              50
    60           70
                               (frames 27 to 30)
```

21.
```
1.123456E+6        1123456.
1.123456E+12       1123456000000.
7.777777E-2        .07777777
1.000000E-12       .000000000001        (frames 45 to 48)
```

CHAPTER TWO

Warming Up

This chapter introduces some of the most used and useful BASIC statements. From here on, more interesting programs may be used as examples, some of which may have application in the preparation of reports or studies required in college courses in the social sciences, psychometrics and testing, and in business.

In this chapter you can learn the function and format for the following BASIC statements, and will practice writing short computer programs. You will also learn and use the concept of *variable* and be able to assign values to those variables in BASIC programming.

| LET | INPUT | GO TO |
| READ | DATA | REMARK |

When you have finished this chapter, you will be able to:

- write short programs where values are assigned to variables by means of LET statements, INPUT statements, and the READ/DATA combination of statements, all expressed in correct BASIC format and notation;

- write short programs where a value calculated by a BASIC expression is assigned to a variable in a LET statement;

- construct a combination of statements to identify the value(s) called for by an INPUT statement;

- write programs that use the GO TO statement to construct a repeated "loop" in some portion of a program (or to "skip over" a portion of a program).

1.   To illustrate the concept of *variable* and the function of the LET statement in BASIC, imagine that there are 26 little boxes inside the computer. Each box can contain one number at any one time:

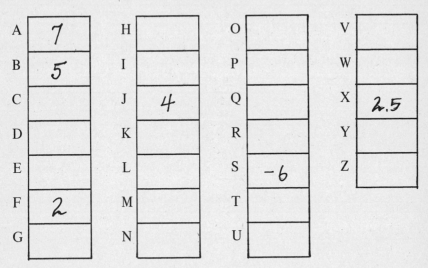

We have already stored numbers in some of the boxes. For example,

    7 is in box A

    5 is in box B

What number is in box F? _____ In J? _____

−6 is in box _____ and 2.5 is in box _____

————————————————————————

    2
    4
    S
    X

2.   Boxes C and N are shown again below. Use a *pencil* to do the following.

(a)   Put 8 into Box C. In other words, write the numeral "8" in the box labeled "C."

(b)   Put 12 into N.

(c)   Put 27 into N. But wait! A box can hold only one number at a time. Before you can enter 27 into N, you must first erase the 12 that you previously entered.

— —

3.   When the computer puts a number into a box, it *automatically* erases the previous content of the box, just as you did. In order to put "27" into Box N, you first erased the previous content, "12."

We call A, B, C, . . . , Z *variables*. The number in Box A is the *value of A;* the number in Box B is the *value of B;* the number in C the *value of C* and so on.

Below is a program that uses the LET statement to instruct the computer to "put a number in a box," or more technically, to assign a numerical *value* to a *variable*. This program tells the computer to

```
10 LET A=7   ← Put 7 into Box A.
20 PRINT A   ← Print the content of Box A
99 END
RUN

    7
```

In the preceding program, the *variable* is _____ and the *value* assigned to it in Line 10 is _____ .

_____

A
7

4.   Complete the following program to assign the value 23 to the variable X and then print the value of X.

    10 _____
    20 _____
    99 END

_____

```
10 LET X=23
20 PRINT X
99 END
RUN

   23
```

5.   Here is another example. This program adds four numbers, which might be scores of some kind, and computes the mean (average).

```
10 LET A=5
20 LET B=8
30 LET C=3
40 LET D=6
50 PRINT "SCORES:";A;B;C;D     ← Print the four scores
60 PRINT "MEAN:";(A+B+C+D)/4   ← Compute and print the mean
99 END
RUN

SCORES: 5  8  3  6
MEAN: 5.5
```

What do the LET statements in this program tell the computer to do? _____

_____

_____

————————————————————————————

Assign numerical values to variables, in this case to put values 5, 8, 3 and 6 into boxes A, B, C, and D. These values are printed (Line 50) and then the computer uses them (Line 60) to compute and print the mean.

6.   Complete each of the following RUNs as you think the computer would do it. If possible, use a computer to find out if you are correct.

(a)
```
10 LET A=1
20 LET A=2
30 PRINT A
99 END
RUN
```
_____

(b)
```
10 LET A=7
20 LET B=A
30 PRINT B
99 END
RUN
```
_____

(c)
```
10 LET A=1
20 PRINT A
30 LET A=2
40 PRINT A
99 END
RUN
```
_____
_____

————————————————————————————

(a) 2   ← *Note that the second value assigned to A in Line 20*
(b) 7   *replaced the value assigned to A by Line 10.*
(c) 1
     2

7.   Look at programs (a), (b), and (c) in the preceding frame. In which program is the value of one variable used to assign a value to another variable?

_____

————————————————————————

program (b)

8.   So it turns out that one variable can take its value from another variable. Not only that, but a variable can get its value from *computations* involving one or more other variables *whose values have been previously assigned*. (That last part is important.)

We can illustrate this with a program that will calculate the grade point average for a student. Assume the student received:

4 units of A
6 units of B
4 units of C
2 units of D
0 units of F

```
100 REMARK GRADE PØINT AVERAGE PRØGRAM USING LET STATEMENTS
110 LET A=4
120 LET B=6 ⎫  These statements tell how many units
130 LET C=4 ⎬  of each grade the student received
140 LET D=2 ⎭
150 LET ,F=0
160 LET U=A+B+C+D+F
170 LET G=(4*A+3*B+2*C+1*D)/U
180 PRINT "YØUR GRADE PØINT AVERAGE IS";G
999 END

RUN

YØUR GRADE PØINT AVERAGE IS 2.75
```

Look at Line 160. Here, U (for units) receives its value from the total of the units of each letter grade. What numerical value does U receive when this program is RUN? U = _____ .

Which line of the program computes and assigns the *computed value* to the variable G? Line _____ .

————————————————————————

U = 16
Line 170

9.   LET statements are all fine and good, but what a hassle to change all those LET statements in Lines 110 to 150 everytime you want to calculate the GPA (Grade Point Average) for a different set of grades. Ah, but leave it to BASIC to come up with a clever solution — namely the INPUT statement.

The INPUT statement allows the computer user to assign *different* values to INPUT variables each time a program is RUN *without* modifying the program itself. When the computer comes to an INPUT statement in a program, it types a question mark and waits for the user to enter a value for the INPUT variables (or variable). Here is an example.

```
20  INPUT A
30  PRINT "THIS TIME A =";A
99  END

RUN

?
```

After we type RUN and press the RETURN key, the computer types a question mark. Then it just waits. What it's waiting for is a value to assign to the INPUT variable A. The computer user must supply a number by *typing the number after the question mark,* and then pressing RETURN.

In our example, we typed in 3 as the value to be assigned to A, pressed RETURN, and the computer then continued running the program, using A = 3. Here's the program again with the completed RUN:

```
20  INPUT A
30  PRINT "THIS TIME A =";A
99  END

RUN

?3
THIS TIME A = 3
```

The *value* of A is printed after the string

After we typed RUN and pressed the RETURN key, the computer typed a

_____ . We then typed a 3, which is our value for

the INPUT variable _____ . The computer then printed the string "THIS

TIME A =" followed by the numerical _____ of A.

_____

    question mark
    A
    value

10. The program can be RUN again with a different value of A supplied by
the user. Show how a RUN would look if the user typed 7 as the value of A.

    RUN

    _____

    _____

_____

    RUN

    ?7
    THIS TIME A = 7

11. Now, in order to make things really clear when dealing with INPUT statements, we need a way of informing the user what the INPUT statement is asking for. Let's add this statement to our example program:

```
10 PRINT "WHAT IS YØUR VALUE FØR A";
```

See the semicolon at the end of the PRINT statement? When a semicolon is used at the end of a PRINT statement, the teletype stays on the same line *instead of* performing a "carriage return" and going to the beginning of the next line. Here is our revised program, and the beginning of a RUN.

```
10 PRINT "WHAT IS YØUR VALUE FØR A";
20 INPUT A
30 PRINT "THIS TIME A =";A
99 END

RUN

WHAT IS YØUR VALUE FØR A?
```

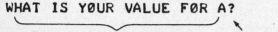

This much comes from Line 10   The question mark comes from
                                      the INPUT statement in Line 20

Now we know exactly what the computer is waiting for — a value for the variable A. We use 350 as the value, type it in after the question mark, then press RETURN.

```
RUN

WHAT IS YØUR VALUE FØR A?350
THIS TIME A = 350
```

Show another RUN of the program where the user enters 17 as the value of A.

```
RUN
```

_____

_____

```
RUN

WHAT IS YØUR VALUE FØR A?17
THIS TIME A = 17
```

12. Now you do one. Write a program, using *two* INPUT statements, that will result in the following printout when RUN.

```
RUN

VALUE ØF X?5          Values supplied by user
VALUE ØF Y?10
THEN X + Y = 15       Value computed
```

Either of these two programs is correct.

```
10 PRINT "VALUE ØF X";        10 PRINT "VALUE ØF X";
20 INPUT X                    20 INPUT X
30 PRINT "VALUE ØF Y";        30 PRINT "VALUE ØF Y";
40 INPUT Y                    40 INPUT Y
50 PRINT "THEN X + Y =";X + Y 50 LET Z = X + Y
99 END                        60 PRINT "THEN X + Y =";Z
RUN                           99 END
                              RUN
VALUE ØF X?5
VALUE ØF Y?10                 VALUE ØF X?5
THEN X + Y = 15               VALUE ØF Y?10
                              THEN X + Y = 15
```

13.   So much for theory. Now let's apply the capabilities of the INPUT statement to the Grade Point Average program (which you may recall seeing at the beginning of Chapter One).

```
100 REMARK PRØGRAM TØ CØMPUTE GRADE PØINT AVERAGE
110 PRINT "HØW MANY UNITS ØF A";
120 INPUT A
130 PRINT "HØW MANY UNITS ØF B";
140 INPUT B
150 PRINT "HØW MANY UNITS ØF C";
160 INPUT C
170 PRINT "HØW MANY UNITS ØF D";
180 INPUT D
190 PRINT "HØW MANY UNITS ØF F";
200 INPUT F
210 LET U=A+B+C+D+F
220 LET G=(4*A+3*B+2*C+1*D)/U
230 PRINT
240 PRINT "YØUR GRADE PØINT AVERAGE IS";G
999 END
```

A PRINT statement with nothing following it causes the teletype to advance to the next line without printing anything, leaving "line spaces" as you can see in the RUN below.

Here is a RUN of the preceding program featuring values of A, B, C, D and F supplied by the user.

```
RUN

HØW MANY UNITS ØF A?4          Following each question mark,
HØW MANY UNITS ØF B?6          the user typed the requested
HØW MANY UNITS ØF C?6          value, then pressed the RETURN
HØW MANY UNITS ØF D?0          key
HØW MANY UNITS ØF F?0

YØUR GRADE PØINT AVERAGE IS 2.875
```

                                    After all 5 values had been entered, the computer
                                    computed the GPA and printed it

How many units of A did the user enter? _____ How many units of
F? _____ .

4
0

14. Let's demonstrate another capability of the INPUT statement. One INPUT statement can be used to assign values of *two or more* variables:

```
10 PRINT "VALUES ØF X AND Y";
20 INPUT X,Y
30 PRINT "THEN X + Y =";X + Y
99 END

RUN

VALUES ØF X AND Y?12,6
THEN X + Y = 18
```

There are two things to note:

(a)   **20 INPUT X,Y**   ← No comma after the last variable

                  ↑ ↖

      No comma here   Comma separates the variables

(b)   **RUN**

     VALUES ØF X AND Y?12,6   ← No comma after last value

                     ↑

                Comma between values

Note that 12 is the value assigned to the first INPUT variable X, and 6 will be assigned to the second INPUT variable Y.

Here is the summary; you fill in the blanks.

When a program containing an INPUT statement with multiple variables is RUN, the first value typed in by the user after the INPUT question mark

will be assigned to the _____ variable that appears in the INPUT

statement; the _____ value typed in by the user will be assigned to the second variable appearing in the INPUT statement, etc. Both the variables in the INPUT statement in the program, *and* the values typed in

by the user when the program is RUN, must be separated by _____ .

_ _

    first
    second
    commas

15. Here is another RUN of the program in frame 14. We want to enter 73 as the value of X and 59 as the value of Y.

RUN

VALUES ØF X AND Y?73   Whoops! We absentmindedly
?   hit the RETURN key.

    The computer typed another question mark.
    This means "Didn't you forget something?"

We then completed the RUN by entering the *second* number, the value of Y. Here is the complete RUN:

RUN

VALUES ØF X AND Y?73
? 59
THEN X + Y = 132

If we don't enter a numerical value for *every* variable in an INPUT statement, *our* computer types a _____.

_____

question mark   (Then we can enter the rest of the required values)

16. Your turn. Write a program to compute and print the value of A*(B+C) for INPUT values of A, B, and C. A RUN should look like the following.

```
RUN

VALUES ØF A,B,C?2,3,4
THEN A*(B + C) = 14
```

Your program:

_____

Here are two ways to do it.

```
10 PRINT "VALUES ØF A,B,C";
20 INPUT A,B,C
30 PRINT "THEN A*(B + C) =";A*(B + C)
99 END

10 PRINT "VALUES ØF A,B,C";
20 INPUT A,B,C
30 LET D=A*(B + C)
40 PRINT "THEN A*(B + C) =";D
99 END
```

17. Now, write a new version of the program to calculate Grade Point Average that uses only one INPUT statement to tell the computer how many units of A, B, C, D, and F you received (or expect to receive). Use a PRINT statement before the INPUT statement to identify the INPUT values needed.

```
100 REMARK PRØGRAM TØ CØMPUTE GRADE PØINT AVERAGE
110 PRINT "UNITS ØF A,B,C,D AND F";
120 INPUT A,B,C,D,F
130 LET U=A+B+C+D+F
140 LET G=(4*A+3*B+2*C+1*D)/U
150 PRINT
160 PRINT "YØUR GRADE PØINT AVERAGE IS";G
999 END
```

You may have noticed the REMARK statement used as a heading for various example programs. That's what it is, a remark by the programmer to identify what a program or a section of a program does. REMARK statements exist solely for the convenience of a person looking at a program, and (for a change) don't tell the computer to do anything. We will use REMARK to identify most of the programs that follow.

18. Now show what a RUN of your program will look like if we enter 2 units of A, 5 units of B, 4 units of C, 3 units of D, and 3 units of F.

RUN

UNITS ØF A,B,C,D AND F?2,5,4,3,3

YØUR GRADE PØINT AVERAGE IS 2

19. Now, let's consider a problem in the field of population growth.

PROBLEM: In year zero, we start with a population of P people. The population increases by 1% each year. In N years, what will the population be?

P is the initial population.
R is the growth rate in percent per year.
N is the number of years.
Q is the population after N years.

$$Q = P(1 + 1/100)^N$$

with labels: 1% increase per year; N years; Initial population; Population at the end of N years.

If the growth rate is 2.5% per year, then

$$Q = P(1 + 2.5/100)^N$$

And, if the growth rate is R% per year, then

$$Q = P(1 + R/100)^N$$

For review, write this last formula as a LET statement for variable Q using
BASIC notation.

     170 LET Q = _____

_____

170 LET Q=P*(1 + R/100)↑N

*NOTE: This formula may actually be used to compute the growth rate for
anything that increases by a fixed proportion or percentage for a given length
of time (e.g., interest on money, bacteria culture growth, etc.).*

20. Here is one version of a population growth program.

```
100 REMARK PRØGRAM TØ CALCULATE PØPULATIØN GRØWTH
110 PRINT "INITIAL PØPULATIØN";
120 INPUT P
130 PRINT "RATE ØF GRØWTH";
140 INPUT R
150 PRINT "NUMBER ØF YEARS";
160 INPUT N
170 LET Q=P*(1+R/100)+N
180 PRINT
190 PRINT "PØPULATIØN AFTER";N;"YEARS IS";Q
999 END

RUN

INITIAL PØPULATIØN?1000
RATE ØF GRØWTH?1
NUMBER ØF YEARS?20

PØPULATIØN AFTER 20 YEARS IS 1220.19
```
                                        ↖
                              We'll call it 1220 people

It is now the year 1978. The population of the earth is about 4.1 billion
people. The growth rate is about 2% per year. Suppose this growth rate
persists until the year 2001. We want to know what the population will be
in 2001. Show how this information is entered by completing the blanks
in the following part of a RUN.

```
RUN

INITIAL PØPULATIØN?_____
RATE ØF GRØWTH?_____
NUMBER ØF YEARS?_____
```

We think you did it this way.

RUN

```
INITIAL POPULATION?4100000000 ←  4.1 billion = 4 100 000 000
RATE OF GROWTH?2
NUMBER OF YEARS?23            ◄──────── 23 = 2001 − 1978

POPULATION AFTER   23   YEARS IS 6.46529E+09
```

Or perhaps this way:

RUN

```
INITIAL POPULATION?4.1E9   ← 4.1 billion = 4.1E9
RATE OF GROWTH?2
NUMBER OF YEARS?23

POPULATION AFTER   23   YEARS IS 6.46529E+09
```

21. According to our RUN in frame 20, in the year 2001 the population of the earth will be 6.46529E+09 people. Here is another way to write that number.

6.46529 billion

Now, you write it in good old everyday, people-type notation.

_____

- -

6,465,290,000, or 6465290000

22. We could, of course, combine the INPUT variables P, R, and N into one INPUT statement.

```
INPUT P,R,N
```

Use the above INPUT statement (you choose the line number) in a new program to compute population growth. A RUN might look like this.

```
RUN

PØPULATIØN, RATE ØF GRØWTH, NUMBER ØF YEARS?1000,1,20

PØPULATIØN AFTER 20 YEARS IS 1220.19
```

```
100 REMARK PRØGRAM TØ CALCULATE PØPULATIØN GRØWTH
110 PRINT "PØPULATIØN, RATE ØF GRØWTH, NUMBER ØF YEARS";
120 INPUT P,R,N
130 LET Q=P*(1+R/100)↑N
140 PRINT
150 PRINT "PØPULATIØN AFTER";N;"YEARS IS";Q
999 END
```

23.   Suppose you and a bunch of friends are gathered around the computer terminal, and they are marvelling at your newly acquired computer programming skills. You decide to demonstrate how the computer works by using the program to calculate GPAs shown in the answer to frame 17. However, you have to do a separate RUN of the program for each friend. But wait — first add these two new statements to the program.

```
170 PRINT
180 GØ TØ 110
```

Now, LIST the program.

```
LIST

100 REMARK PRØGRAM TØ CØMPUTE GRADE PØINT AVERAGE
110 PRINT "UNITS ØF A,B,C,D AND F";
120 INPUT A,B,C,D,F
130 LET U=A+B+C+D+F
140 LET G=(4*A+3*B+2*C+1*D)/U
150 PRINT
160 PRINT "YØUR GRADE PØINT AVERAGE IS";G
170 PRINT
180 GØ TØ 110
999 END
```

In BASIC, the GO TO statement instructs the computer to "jump" forward or backward in the program to the line number indicated after the GO TO, and then to continue following the instructions in the program *in line number order from that point.*

In the preceding example, the GO TO statement tells the computer to jump from Line 180 to Line _____ and start the program over again.

————————————————————————

   Line 110

NOTE: Although the END statement (Line 999) is never executed, in most versions of BASIC it must still be included simply to mark the end of the program.

24. What is the purpose of Line 170 in the preceding program?

_____

_____

– –

It causes the computer to print a line space after printing the grade point average.

25. Let's see what happens when the program is RUN.

RUN

```
UNITS ØF A,B,C,D AND F?4,6,4,2,0
                          Don't forget the zero for no units of F.
YØUR GRADE PØINT AVERAGE IS 2.75

UNITS ØF A,B,C,D AND F?10,22,12,8,4
                          This friend wants the GPA for 4 semesters
YØUR GRADE PØINT AVERAGE IS 2.464286

UNITS ØF A,B,C,D AND F?12,3,0,0,0

YØUR GRADE PØINT AVERAGE IS 3.8   This friend is a genius

UNITS ØF A,B,C,D AND F?0,0,3,10,2

YØUR GRADE PØINT AVERAGE IS 1.066667
                          This friend is on probation!
UNITS ØF A,B,C,D AND F?     What again?
```

The computer still wants more data. How do you get out of this situation? Try these methods: Type STOP and press RETURN. If that doesn't work, hold the CTRL key down and press the C key. Then let go and press RE- TURN, or try the BREAK key.

If that doesn't work, press the ESC or ALT MODE key. If that doesn't work, ask for help or consult the reference manual for the system being used. (If you haven't guessed, various computer systems use different methods to abort an INPUT statement. Later you'll learn programming techniques to avoid this problem.)

Different computers may use different ways to abort or terminate an INPUT statement. If these don't work on your computer, what should you do?

_____

_____

    Yell for help.
    Consult your local reference manual   (Either answer is O.K.)

26.   Below is a population growth program.

```
100 REMARK PRØGRAM TØ CALCULATE PØPULATIØN GRØWTH
110 PRINT "PØPULATIØN, RATE ØF GRØWTH, NUMBER ØF YEARS";
120 INPUT P,R,N
130 LET Q=P*(1+R/100)↑N
140 PRINT
150 PRINT "PØPULATIØN AFTER";N;"YEARS IS";Q
999 END
```

Modify the program so that, after printing the result for input values of P, R, and N, the computer returns to Line 110. Also include a statement to put a line space following the printed results. Show your modifications below.

_____

_____

_____

Here is a LIST and RUN of the modified program.

```
LIST

100 REMARK PRØGRAM TØ CALCULATE PØPULATIØN GRØWTH
110 PRINT "PØPULATIØN, RATE ØF GRØWTH, NUMBER ØF YEARS";
120 INPUT P,R,N
130 LET Q=P*(1+R/100)↑N
140 PRINT
150 PRINT "PØPULATIØN AFTER";N;"YEARS IS";Q
160 PRINT◀━━━━ Here are the modifications
170 GØ TØ 110◀━
999 END

RUN

PØPULATIØN, RATE ØF GRØWTH, NUMBER ØF YEARS?1000,1,20

PØPULATIØN AFTER 20 YEARS IS 1220.19

PØPULATIØN, RATE ØF GRØWTH, NUMBER ØF YEARS?1000,2,20

PØPULATIØN AFTER 20 YEARS IS 1485.947

PØPULATIØN, RATE ØF GRØWTH, NUMBER ØF YEARS?    And so on
```

27. Here's a program that lets you use the computer as an adding machine, by repeating an "adding routine" with a GO TO loop.

```
100 REMARK WØRLD'S MØST EXPENSIVE ADDING MACHINE
110 PRINT "I AM THE WØRLD'S MØST EXPENSIVE ADDING MACHINE."
120 PRINT "EACH TIME I TYPE 'X=?' THEN YØU TYPE A NUMBER AND"

130 PRINT "PRESS THE RETURN KEY. I WILL PRINT THE TØTAL ØF ALL"
140 PRINT "THE NUMBERS YØU HAVE ENTERED."
150 LET T=0

160 PRINT                          Lines 160 through 210 are a
170 PRINT "X=";                     GO TO loop. These lines are
180 INPUT X                         done for each input number
190 LET T=T+X
200 PRINT "TØTAL SØ FAR IS";T
210 GØ TØ 160

999 END
```

Note the LET statements using the variable T in Lines 150 and 190.

150 LET T=0   190 LET T=T+X

Line 150 is *outside* the GO TO loop. It is done *once* before the loop begins, setting T equal to zero. This is called "initializing," giving an initial or start- ing value to a variable.

Line 190 is *inside* the GO TO loop. Therefore, it will be done each time through the loop. In Line 190, a *new* value for T is computed by adding the *old* value to T and the INPUT value of X.

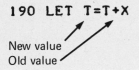

190 LET T=T+X

New value
Old value

(a)   Suppose the *old* value of T is zero and the INPUT value of X is 12.

What is the *new* value of T? _____

(b)   Suppose the *old* value of T is 12 and the INPUT value of X is 43.

What is the *new* value of T? _____

12
55

28. Note how PRINT statements (Lines 110 – 140) are used to provide the user with an explanation and instructions for using the program. These

PRINT statements are _____ the GO TO loop.
                      (inside/outside)

_____

outside

29. Now, let's RUN the program and see how it works.

RUN

```
I AM THE WØRLD'S MØST EXPENSIVE ADDING MACHINE.
EACH TIME I TYPE 'X=?' THEN YØU TYPE A NUMBER AND
PRESS THE RETURN KEY. I WILL PRINT THE TØTAL ØF ALL
THE NUMBERS YØU HAVE ENTERED.

X=?12
TØTAL SØ FAR IS 12

X=?43
TØTAL SØ FAR IS 55

X=?33
TØTAL SØ FAR IS 88

X=?92
TØTAL SØ FAR IS 180

X=?76.25
TØTAL SØ FAR IS 256.25

X=?   ← Do you remember how to get out of this?
          (If not, check frame 25.)
```

For the preceding RUN, the *first* time through the program, the values of
the variables on the right of the = symbol in 190 LET T = T + X will be

LET T = 0 + 12

↑   ↑

Value assigned to   Value assigned to X
T by Line 150   by INPUT

So the new value of T is 12.

For the *second* time through the "loop" section of the program, show
the values:

LET T = _____ + _____

So the new value of T is _____.

_____

12
43   (LET T = 12 + 43)
55

30. You've seen how LET statements and INPUT statements can be used to assign values to variables. (We hope you've been able to use them at a terminal too.) A third method uses two statements in combination, READ and DATA, to assign values to variables.

```
10 READ X
20 PRINT "THIS TIME THROUGH THE LOOP, X=";X
30 GO TO 10
40 DATA 10, 15, 7, 3.25, 11
99 END

RUN

THIS TIME THROUGH THE LOOP, X= 10
THIS TIME THROUGH THE LOOP, X= 15
THIS TIME THROUGH THE LOOP, X= 7
THIS TIME THROUGH THE LOOP, X= 3.25
THIS TIME THROUGH THE LOOP, X= 11

OUT OF DATA IN LINE 10
```

This statement

```
10 READ X
```

tells the computer to READ one value from the DATA statement, and assign the value to the variable X. Everytime the READ statement is executed (each time through the loop), the computer reads the next value from the DATA statement, and assigns the new value to the variable X. The computer keeps track of each value as it is read out, in effect, moving a pointer down the line of numbers in the DATA statement, one notch at a time.

How many numbers are in the DATA statement? _____

_____

5

31. The computer read and printed all the numbers in the DATA statement then tried to find still another number. Since it couldn't find another number to read, what did it print?

_____

_____

    ØUT ØF DATA IN LINE 10

32. Look at the format for DATA statements:

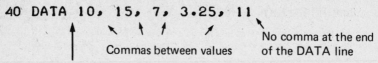

40 DATA 10, 15, 7, 3.25, 11

Commas between values

No comma at the end
of the DATA line

No comma here

CAN   *DATA statements may contain whole numbers, numbers with decimal fractions, such as 3.25 above, numbers in scientific or "E" notation, or negative numbers.*

CAN'T   *DATA statements may not contain variables, arithmetic operations, other functions, or fractions.*

90 DATA X,Y,A   (Well, at least most computers CAN'T.
95 DATA 2+3,1/4,2/5,7*8 What about yours? Try it and find out.)

Write a DATA statement for these values:

    342
    1256
    205
    60.25
    −412
    2.05E8

---

60 DATA 342,1256,205,60.25,−412,2.05E8

(Remember, no commas can be used in large numbers.
However, scientific or "E" notation may be used.)

Your line
number
may be
different

33. Notice that the DATA statement may be placed anywhere in the program (before the END statement).

```
10  READ X                      10  READ X
15  DATA 3,0,5,7,5,2,-1         20  PRINT "X=";X
20  PRINT "X=";X                30  GØ TØ 10
30  GØ TØ 10                    70  DATA 3,0,5,7,5,2,-1
99  END                         99  END
RUN                             RUN
```

```
    X= 3                            X= 3        Since Line 10 tells the
    X= 0                            X= 0        computer to READ X,
    X= 5                            X= 5        the computer will find
    X= 7                            X= 7        the DATA statement
    X= 5                            X= 5        (Line 70) read one
    X= 2                            X= 2        number (into X) then
    X=-1                            X=-1        proceed to Line 20,
                                                and so on.

ØUT ØF DATA IN LINE 10      ØUT ØF DATA IN LINE 10
```

Can the DATA statement be placed as shown below?

```
(a)  5  DATA 3,0,5,7,5,2,-1    (b)  10  READ X
     10  READ X                     20  PRINT "X=";X
     20  PRINT "X=";X               30  GØ TØ 10
     30  GØ TØ 10                   99  END
     99  END                        100 DATA 3,0,5,7,5,2,-1
```

answer_____   answer _____

_____

(a) Yes.
(b) No. The line number of the DATA statement cannot be larger than the line number of the END statement.

34. As many DATA statements as are needed may be used to hold the data. Sometimes you may wish to use a DATA statement to hold only one value that you expect to change for various RUNS of the program. Sometimes you may have more values than will fit on one line. When the computer has used all the data in one DATA statement, it automatically goes on to the next DATA statement, and continues reading values. But each new DATA statement must begin with a new line number and the word DATA.

```
10  READ X
20  PRINT "X=";X
30  GO TO 10
70  DATA 3,0,5,7
75  DATA 5,2,-1
99  END

RUN

X=  3
X=  0
X=  5
X=  7
X=  5
X=  2
X=-1


OUT OF DATA IN LINE 10
```

If the computer has already used up all the numbers in all the DATA statements in a program and then tries to read another number, it will type an error message and stop. Typical error messages are

OF OF DATA   or   DATA ERROR

or some other indication that it can find no more DATA to assign to the READ variable.

What message did our computer print when it could find no more data to assign to the READ variable?

_____

_____

```
OUT OF DATA IN LINE 10
```

35. Write a "World's Most Expensive Adding Machine" program (from frame 27) using READ and DATA statements instead of an INPUT statement so that a RUN of the program will look like this:

```
RUN

X= 12
TOTAL SO FAR IS 12        Examine the RUN to determine
                          the values in the DATA statement

X= 43
TOTAL SO FAR IS 55

X= 33
TOTAL SO FAR IS 88

X= 92
TOTAL SO FAR IS 180

X= 76.25
TOTAL SO FAR IS 256.25

OUT OF DATA IN LINE 30
                         ⌐── This may be different
                             for your program
```

```
10 REMARK WORLD'S MOST EXPENSIVE ADDING MACHINE REVISITED
20 LET T=0
30 READ X
40 LET T=T+X
50 PRINT "X=";X
60 PRINT "TOTAL SO FAR IS";T
70 PRINT
80 GO TO 30
90 DATA 12,43,33,92,76.25
99 END
```

36. Find the "Program to Calculate Population Growth" (frame 26). In that program, the INPUT statement looks like this:

```
120 INPUT P,R,N
```

Similarly, a READ statement can assign successive values from a DATA statement to a series of READ variables:

```
120 READ P,R,N
```

The format is like the INPUT statement with multiple variables — the variables are separated by commas, with *no comma after* READ *or* after the last variable.

```
100 REMARK PRØGRAM TØ CALCULATE PØPULATIØN GRØWTH
110 READ P,R
115 DATA 1000,1
120 PRINT "INITIAL PØPULATIØN IS";P
130 PRINT "GRØWTH RATE IS";R;"%"
140 PRINT
150 READ N
155 DATA 10,20,50,100
160 LET Q=P*(1+R/100)↑N
170 PRINT "PØPULATIØN AFTER";N;"YEARS IS";Q
180 GØ TØ 150
999 END
RUN

INITIAL PØPULATIØN IS 1000 ← Values assigned to P and R
GRØWTH RATE IS 1 %        ←        by Line 110

PØPULATIØN AFTER 10 YEARS IS 1104.622
PØPULATIØN AFTER 20 YEARS IS 1220.19
PØPULATIØN AFTER 50 YEARS IS 1644.631
PØPULATIØN AFTER 100 YEARS IS 2704.811

ØUT ØF DATA IN LINE 150
```

To help clarify what happens when this program is RUN, we have placed the DATA statements near the READ statements. However, the DATA statements (Lines 115 and 155) could be combined into one DATA statement, which could be placed anywhere in the program. The first two values from the combined DATA statement would be assigned to the READ variables P and R in Line 110, and the remaining values would be assigned (one at a time) to N in Line 150, with one value used each time through the GO TO loop.

Now combine the two DATA statements in the preceding program into a single DATA statement and write it as Line 900.

900 _____

_____

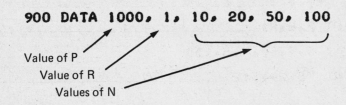

900 DATA 1000, 1, 10, 20, 50, 100

Value of P
Value of R
Values of N

37. After removing Lines 115 and 155 from the new population growth program, Line 900 is added to the program. How will these changes affect the RUN of the program?

_____

_____

There will be no effect on the RUN; it will be the same as before. (Try it and see for yourself.)

SELF-TEST

If you can successfully deal with the following problems, you have the first
two chapters down pat. If you have trouble, you'd better review the first
two chapters before going on. (Have you been writing out the answers before
looking at ours? That's the best way to learn from this text.)

1. Each of the following BASIC statements contains an error. Mark the
   error and show the statement in correct BASIC notation.

   (a) `10  READ X;Y` _____

   (b) `10  "X+Y=";X+Y` _____

   (c) `30  LET X+3 = Y` _____

   (d) `20  INPUT P,Q,R,` _____

   (e) `90  DATA, 5.5,50,7.5,100` _____

   (f) `10  PRINT "S↑2=;S↑2` _____

2. Each of the following BASIC programs contains an error. In the space
   provided, describe the error.

   (a)
   ```
   10  READ A,B
   20  PRINT A+B
   99  END
   ```
   _____

   (b)
   ```
   10  INPUT X,Y
   20  PRINT X*Y
   30  GO TO 10
   ```
   _____

   (c)
   ```
   10  LET P=5
   20  LET Q=22
   30  LET S=(P+Q)/(Q-R)
   40  PRINT M,N,S
   99  END
   ```
   _____

3.   Look at this short program. What will the computer print when the

program is RUN? _____

Why? _____

```
10 LET R=15
20 GO TO 99
30 PRINT R
99 END
```

4.   Write a program that will convert temperatures expressed in degrees
Celsius to degrees Fahrenheit, using this formula:

$$F = 9/5C + 32$$

A RUN of your program should look like this:

```
RUN

THIS PROGRAM CONVERTS DEGREES CELSIUS TO FAHRENHEIT.
C =?32
 32 DEGREES C = 89.6 DEGREES F.

C =?80
 80 DEGREES C = 176 DEGREES F.

C =?100
 100 DEGREES C = 212 DEGREES F.

C =?0
 0 DEGREES C = 32 DEGREES F.
```

5. Write a program that will convert the temperatures taken hourly for one
    day from degrees Fahrenheit to degrees Celsius. Use the READ
    and DATA combination of statements in your program, and construct
    your program to produce the following RUN.

RUN   Formula: $C = 5/9(F - 32)$

```
F = 52        C = 11.11111
F = 51        C = 10.55556
F = 51        C = 10.55556
F = 53        C = 11.66667
F = 54        C = 12.22222
F = 60        C = 15.55556
F = 64        C = 17.77778
F = 68        C = 20
F = 73        C = 22.77778
F = 79        C = 26.11111
F = 82        C = 27.77778
F = 83        C = 28.33333
F = 85        C = 29.44444
F = 87        C = 30.55556
F = 84        C = 28.88889
F = 83        C = 28.33333
F = 80        C = 26.66667
F = 75        C = 23.88889
F = 69        C = 20.55556
F = 65        C = 18.33333
F = 63        C = 17.22222
F = 60        C = 15.55556
F = 59        C = 15
F = 57        C = 13.88889

OUT OF DATA IN LINE 10
```

6. Congratulations! You are the big winner on a TV show. Your prize is selected as follows.

A number between 10 and 1000 is chosen at random. Call it N. You then select one and only one of the following prizes.

PRIZE NO. 1: You receive N dollars.
PRIZE NO. 2: You receive D dollars where D is computed as follows:

$$D = 1.01^N$$

Perhaps you recognize the formula for D. It is the amount that you would receive if you invested $1 at 1% interest per day, compounded daily for N days.

The question, of course, is: For a given value of N, which prize do you take, PRIZE NO. 1 or PRIZE NO. 2? Write a program to help you decide. A RUN of your program should look like this:

```
RUN

N=? 100
PRIZE #1 = $ 100          PRIZE #2 =$ 2.70481
              (Take PRIZE NO. 1)


N=? 500
PRIZE #1 = $ 500          PRIZE #2 =$ 144.7717
              (Take PRIZE NO. 1)


N=? 1000
PRIZE #1 = $ 1000         PRIZE #2 =$ 20958.85

N=? and so on.    (Take PRIZE NO. 2)
```

BONUS PROBLEM. Write a program to help you perform that tiresome task called "balancing the checkbook." Here is a RUN of our program.

```
RUN

I WILL HELP YOU BALANCE YOUR CHECKBOOK.
ENTER CHECKS AS NEGATIVE NUMBERS AND
DEPOSITS AS POSITIVE NUMBERS.

OLD BALANCE? 123.45

CHECK OR DEPOSIT?-3.95 ←——— Remember — enter checks as numbers.
NEW BALANCE: 119.5

CHECK OR DEPOSIT?-33
NEW BALANCE: 86.5

CHECK OR DEPOSIT?-73.69
NEW BALANCE: 13.11

CHECK OR DEPOSIT?-8.24
NEW BALANCE: 4.87

CHECK OR DEPOSIT? 50 ←——— At last! A deposit, and just in time.
NEW BALANCE: 54.87

CHECK OR DEPOSIT?   ...and so on.
```

Answers to Self-Test

The frame numbers in parentheses refer to the frames in the chapter where the topic is discussed. You may wish to refer to these for quick review.

1.
(a) 10 READ X ⓙ Y	10 READ X,Y	(frame 32)
(b) 100"X + Y ="; X + Y	10 PRINT "X + Y ="; X + Y	(frames 9 and 12)
(c) 30 LET (X+3) = Y	30 LET Y=X+3	(frames 1 to 9)
(d) 20 INPUT P, Q, R⑥	20 INPUT P, Q, R	(frame 14)
(e) 90 DATA⑥ 5.5,50,7.5,100	90 DATA 5.5,50,7.5,100	(frame 32)
(f) 10 PRINT "S↑2 =↓ S↑2	10 PRINT "S↑2=";S↑2	(frames 9, 12, and 16)

2. (a) Program lacks DATA statement to go with READ statement. (frames 30 to 37)
    (b) Missing END statement. (frame 23)
    (c) No value has been assigned to variable R used in Line 30 to calculate a value to assign to S. M and N also have no value. (frame 8)

3. Nothing, because the GO TO statement causes the computer to jump past the PRINT statement. (frame 23)

4. *NOTE: Remember that there may be more than one program that will solve the problem and produce the RUN shown. If yours doesn't look like our solution, and you think it will work, try it on a computer.*

```
10 PRINT "THIS PROGRAM CONVERTS DEGREES CELSIUS TO FAHRENHEIT."
20 PRINT "C=";
30 INPUT C
40 LET F=C*9/5+32
50 PRINT C;"DEGREES C =";F;"DEGREES F."
60 PRINT
70 GO TO 20
99 END
```

(frames 12 and 20)

5.
```
10 READ F
20 LET C=5/9*(F-32)
30 PRINT "F =";F,"C =";C
40 GO TO 10
90 DATA 52,51,51,53,54,60,64,68,73,79,82,83
91 DATA 85,87,84,83,80,75,69,65,63,60,59,57
99 END
```
(frame 30)

6.
```
10 PRINT "N=";
20 INPUT N
30 PRINT "PRIZE#1 = $";N,"PRIZE"2 = $";1.01↑N
40 PRINT
50 GO TO 10
99 END
```
(frame 12)

CHAPTER THREE
Decision Making

Onward into conditional branching and the IF-THEN statement. The more BASIC you learn, the more control you have over the capabilities of computers.

When you complete this chapter, you will be able to:

- write programs correctly using the IF-THEN statement for conditional branching, with any of the following comparisons

        =
        <
        >
        <=
        >=
        <>

- use the IF-THEN statement to check for a "flag" in a program;

- use another form of BASIC variable notation, a letter with a digit.

In this chapter we present a very important computer capability known technically as *conditional branching*. IF a given condition is *true*, THEN the computer branches off, or "skips" to a specified line in the program and continues following the instructions in the program. The BASIC statement used for conditional branching in a program is the IF-THEN statement. The IF part of the statement states the condition, and the THEN part tells the computer where to branch or "skip" to when the IF part is true.

1.   An IF-THEN statement is shown below.

   20 IF X < 0 THEN 10

This IF-THEN statement tells the computer

> If the value of X is less than
> zero then go to Line 10

If the value of X is greater than zero or equal to zero, the computer does not go to Line 10. Instead it simply continues in normal line number order. That is, it goes on to the next line number in the program sequence. In the diagram below follow the arrows.

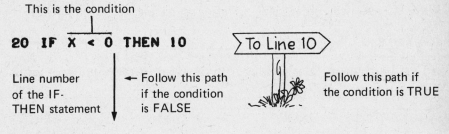

What is the *condition* in the above IF-THEN statement? _____

_____

X < 0 or X is less than zero

The condition is TRUE for some values of X and FALSE for other values of X.

2.   The condition in an IF-THEN statement is usually a comparison between a variable and a number, or between two variables, or in general, a comparison between two BASIC expressions. For example,

The statement: **50 IF A = B THEN 100**

tells the computer: If the value of A is equal to the value of B,
                       then go to Line 100

The statement: **90 IF Q >= 2*P THEN 120**

tells the computer: If the value of Q is greater than or equal to
                       2 times the value of P, then go to Line 120

Here is a handy table of comparison symbols that may be used in an IF-THEN statement:

BASIC Symbol	Comparison	Math Symbol
=	is equal to	$=$
<	is less than	$<$
>	is greater than	$>$
<=	is less than or equal to	$\leq$
>=	is greater than or equal to	$\geq$
<>	is not equal to	$\neq$

Write the following as IF-THEN statements using the proper BASIC symbols.

(a)   If the value of M is less than one then go to Line 50. _____

(b)   If the value of Z is greater than or equal to the value of A squared, then go to Line 150. _____

(c)   If the value of 3 times A is not equal to 12, then go to Line 80.

_____

_____

(a) **IF M < 1 THEN 50**
(b) **IF Z >= A↑2 THEN 150**
(c) **IF 3*A <> 12 THEN 80**

3. The following program causes the computer to read numbers from a DATA statement and print only the numbers that are *not* less than zero. Numbers that are greater than zero or equal to zero *are* printed.

```
10 READ X
20 IF X<0 THEN 10
30 PRINT "X =";X
40 GO TO 10
90 DATA 3,7,0,-2,5,-1,6,8,-3
99 END

RUN

X = 3
X = 7
X = 0
X = 5
X = 6
X = 8

OUT OF DATA IN LINE 10
```

Look at the numbers in the DATA statement. For which numbers is the condition X < 0 true? _____

_____

    −2, −1, −3

4. When X < 0 is true, what line does the computer go to? _____

_____

    Line 10

5. If X < 0 is true, is the value of X printed? _____

_____

    No

6.   For which numbers is the condition X < 0 false? _____

_____

3, 7, 0, 5, 6, 8

7.   When X < 0 is false, what line does the computer go to? _____

_____

Line 30

8.   If X < 0 is false, is the value of X printed? _____

_____

Yes

9.   What will be the results of the following RUN?

```
10 READ X
20 IF X>0 THEN 10
30 PRINT "X =";X
40 GO TO 10
90 DATA 3,7,0,-2,5,-1,6,8,-3
99 END

RUN
```

The condition in the
IF-THEN statement
is X> 0 (X is greater
than zero)

OUT OF DATA IN LINE 10

RUN

X = 0
X =-2
X =-1
X =-3

ØUT ØF DATA IN LINE 10

10. Change the IF-THEN statement in the above program so that only *nonzero* numbers are printed. That is, if X = 0, it is not printed.

20 IF _____ THEN 10

----

20 IF X = 0 THEN 10

11. Change the IF-THEN statement so that only numbers greater than or equal to 3 are printed. That is, if a number is less than 3, it is not printed.

----

20 IF X<3 THEN 10

12. Show the results if we RUN the following program.

```
10 READ X
20 IF X<0 THEN 10
30 PRINT X;
40 GØ TØ 10
90 DATA 5,-3,6,0,8,-1,2,0,6,7
99 END

RUN
```

_____

```
RUN

   5   6   0   8   2   0   6   7

ØUT ØF DATA IN LINE 10
```

13. Rewrite Line 20 so that the results of a RUN are

```
RUN

   5   6   8   2   6   7

ØUT ØF DATA IN LINE 10
20 _____
```

_____

```
20 IF X<=0 THEN 10
```

14. Rewrite Line 20 so that the results of a RUN are

    RUN

    -3 -1

    ØUT ØF DATA IN LINE 10

    20 _____

    _____

    20 IF X>=0 THEN 10

15. Rewrite Line 20 so that the results of a RUN are

    RUN

    0 0

    ØUT ØF DATA IN LINE 10

    20 _____

    _____

    20 IF X<>0 THEN 10

    (If X is *not equal* to zero then go to Line 10)

Remember, in BASIC we use < > to mean "not equal to."

16. Here is another IF-THEN statement.

40 IF X>25 THEN 60

The statement begins with a line number (40). It tells the computer to compare the current value of X with 25, and if X is *greater than* 25, go to Line 60 and continue running the program. If the computer finds that the current value of X is less than or equal to 25, it merely continues on to the next statement in the program (Line 50).

To demonstrate:

```
10 LET X=0
20 PRINT "X =";X
30 LET X=X+5
40 IF X>25 THEN 60
50 GØ TØ 20
60 PRINT
70 PRINT "NØW X =";X;"SØ THE IF-THEN STATEMENT"
80 PRINT "GØT ME ØUT ØF THE LØØP."
99 END

RUN

X = 0
X = 5
X = 10
X = 15
X = 20
X = 25

NØW X = 30 SØ THE IF-THEN STATEMENT
GØT ME ØUT ØF THE LØØP.
```

(a) Which lines comprise a loop in this program? Lines _____.
(b) Which line increased the "old" value of X by 5 each time through the loop? _____
(c) How many times did the IF-THEN statement check the value of X *before* it found the condition set to be true? _____ times.

_____

(a)   Lines 20, 30, 40, 50
(b)   Line 30
(c)   6 times

17. Here is another demonstration of how the IF-THEN statement works.

```
5    REMARK THIS PROGRAM COMPARES TWO NUMBERS
10   PRINT
20   PRINT "INPUT ANY TWO NUMBERS";
30   INPUT A,B
40   IF A<B THEN 70
50   IF A>B THEN 90
60   IF A=B THEN 110
70   PRINT A;"IS LESS THAN ";B
80   GOTO 10
90   PRINT A;"IS GREATER THAN ";B
100  GOTO 10
110  PRINT A;"IS EQUAL TO ";B
120  GOTO 10
999  END
```

RUN

```
INPUT ANY TWO NUMBERS?10,10
 10 IS EQUAL TO 10

INPUT ANY TWO NUMBERS?50000,1
 50000 IS GREATER THAN 1

INPUT ANY TWO NUMBERS?22
?23
 22 IS LESS THAN 23

INPUT ANY TWO NUMBERS?-1,-2
-1 IS GREATER THAN -2

INPUT ANY TWO NUMBERS?-4,0
-4 IS LESS THAN 0
```

If you input only one number, the computer types another question mark

The last set of INPUT values make the condition *true* for which of the three IF-THEN statements? Line _____.

_____

Line 40

18. Which IF-THEN statement, when the condition is true, causes the computer to jump to the line 70 PRINT statement? Line _____.

————————————————————————

   Line 40

19. Here's an exercise in (if you'll excuse the computerese) getting the bugs out of a program. *Debugging* a program means to find out why the program isn't doing what the programmer intended. For the programmer, it means checking the overall design, order, and placement of statements, the use of the programming language, and (last but not least), typing and copying errors made when entering the program.

```
5    REMARK FAULTY PROGRAM #1
10   PRINT
20   PRINT "INPUT ANY TWO NUMBERS";
30   INPUT A,B
40   IF A<B THEN 70
50   IF A>B THEN 80
60   IF A=B THEN 90
70   PRINT A;"IS LESS THAN ";B
80   PRINT A;"IS GREATER THAN ";B
90   PRINT A;"IS EQUAL TO ";B
100   GOTO 10
999   END


RUN

INPUT ANY TWO NUMBERS? 1,1000
 1 IS LESS THAN 1000
 1 IS GREATER THAN 1000
 1 IS EQUAL TO 1000

INPUT ANY TWO NUMBERS? 123,5
 123 IS GREATER THAN 5
 123 IS EQUAL TO 5


INPUT ANY TWO NUMBERS?
```

No, the computer isn't flipped out. It just followed the program

Follow through the preceding program very carefully. How can this program be amended to perform properly?

_____

_____

(If you are at a computer terminal, try your solution instead of looking at the answer below.)

— .

Add these statements.

```
75 GØ TØ 10
85 GØ TØ 10
```

(If you found another solution which you think works, try it on the computer.)

20. Write a program. Your program should direct the computer to determine whether an INPUT value of X is *positive, negative* or *zero* and print an appropriate message. A RUN might look like this:

```
RUN

WHEN I ASK, YOU ENTER A NUMBER AND I WILL TELL YOU
WHETHER YOUR NUMBER IS POSITIVE, NEGATIVE OR ZERO.

WHAT IS YOUR NUMBER?-3
-3 IS NEGATIVE

WHAT IS YOUR NUMBER?0
 0 IS ZERO

WHAT IS YOUR NUMBER?7
 7 IS POSITIVE

WHAT IS YOUR NUMBER?     and so on
```

_____

Here is one solution.

```
100 REMARK DETERMINE IF X IS POSITIVE, NEGATIVE OR ZERO
110 PRINT "WHEN I ASK, YOU ENTER A NUMBER AND I WILL TELL YOU"
120 PRINT "WHETHER YOUR NUMBER IS POSITIVE, NEGATIVE OR ZERO."
130 PRINT
140 PRINT "WHAT IS YOUR NUMBER";
150 INPUT X
160 IF X>0 THEN 190
170 IF X<0 THEN 210
180 IF X=0 THEN 230
190 PRINT X;"IS POSITIVE"
200 GO TO 130
210 PRINT X;"IS NEGATIVE"
220 GO TO 130
230 PRINT X;"IS ZERO"
240 GO TO 130
999 END
```

Lines 160 through 240 in this program can be replaced by the slightly
shorter set of statements shown below.

```
160 IF X>0 THEN 200
170 IF X<0 THEN 220
180 PRINT X;"IS ZERO"   ◄──── If X isn't positive or negative,
190 GO TO 130                  then it's got to be zero
200 PRINT X;"IS POSITIVE"
210 GO TO 130
220 PRINT X;"IS NEGATIVE"
230 GO TO 130
```

21. One common application of the IF-THEN statement involves the use
of a "flag" (signal) that terminates one process and begins another:

```
10    REMARK CØMPUTE MEAN ØF INPUT VALUES
20    PRINT "THIS PRØGRAM CØMPUTES THE MEAN ØF THE VALUES"
30    PRINT "YØU TYPE IN AFTER EACH 'X=?'. WHEN YØU ARE"
40    PRINT "DØNE ENTERING VALUES, TYPE -1 AFTER 'X=?' AND"
50    PRINT "I WILL CØMPUTE THE MEAN."
60    PRINT
70    LET T=0
80    LET N=0
90    PRINT "X=";
100   INPUT X
110   IF X=-1 THEN 150
120   LET T=T+X
130   LET N=N+1
140   GØTØ 90
150   PRINT
160   PRINT "N =";N
170   PRINT "TØTAL =";T
180   PRINT "MEAN =";T/N
999   END

RUN

THIS PRØGRAM CØMPUTES THE MEAN ØF THE VALUES
YØU TYPE IN AFTER EACH 'X=?'. WHEN YØU ARE
DØNE ENTERING VALUES, TYPE -1 AFTER 'X=?' AND
I WILL CØMPUTE THE MEAN.

X=?25
X=?37
X=?42
X=?19
X=?-1

N = 4
TØTAL = 123
MEAN = 30.75
```

The flag used in this program is -1. This statement

110 IF X=-1 THEN 150

checks each input value, and if it is -1, it jumps the computer to Line 150 of the program, and the summary of the data is printed.

Modify the program so that, instead of using -1 for the flag, the operator uses 999999. You will have to change Lines 40 and 110.

40 _____

110 _____

_ _

```
40 PRINT "DØNE ENTERING VALUES, TYPE 999999 AFTER 'X=?' AND"

110 IF X=999999 THEN 150
```

22. Here is how the same system can be used in DATA statements.

```
10   REMARK COMPUTE MEAN OF DATA STATEMENT VALUES
70   LET T=0
80   LET N=0
100  READ X
110  IF X=-1 THEN 150
120  LET T=T+X
130  LET N=N+1
140  GOTO 100
150  PRINT
160  PRINT "N =";N
170  PRINT "TOTAL =";T
180  PRINT "MEAN =";T/N
900  DATA 25,37,42,19,-1
999  END

RUN


N = 4
TOTAL = 123
MEAN = 30.75
```

However, −1 may not be a good flag to use for some data if the values are both positive and negative.

Here are temperatures recorded during one cold week in Minneapolis.

S	M	T	W	TH	F	S
10	3	−9	−15	−23	−25	−30

We want to use the above program to compute the mean temperature for that unpleasant week. Rewrite Lines 110 and 900 for this set of data. Use 999999 as the flag.

110 _____

900 _____

----

110 IF X=999999 THEN 150

900 DATA 10,3,-9,-15,-23,-25,-30,999999

This is an unlikely value, and makes a good flag

23. Questionnaire.

```
┌──────────────────────────────────────────────┐
│  DOES YOUR COMPUTER UNDERSTAND YOU?            │
│                                                │
│               1.  YES                          │
│                                                │
│               2.  NO                           │
└──────────────────────────────────────────────┘
```

We gave this questionnaire to 50 people and got 50 answers. Each answer is 1 (YES) or 2 (NO). The answers are shown below in five DATA statements. The last answer is followed by −1.

```
900    REMARK DATA: 1=YES, 2=NO, -1=END OF DATA
910    DATA 1,2,2,2,1,2,1,2,1,2
920    DATA 2,1,1,1,2,1,2,2,2,1
930    DATA 2,2,2,1,2,1,2,2,1,2
940    DATA 1,1,1,1,2,1,2,2,1,1
950    DATA 2,2,2,2,1,1,1,2,1,2,-1
```

How many YES answers? _____
How many NO answers? _____

Write the number of YES answers in the box labeled "Y" and the number of NO answers in the box labeled "N."

Y ☐

N ☐

---

23 YES answers
27 NO answers

Y ⟨23⟩

N ⟨27⟩

24. Here is a program to read the answers from the DATA statements and count the number of YES answers and NO answers.

The variable Y is used to count YES answers.
The variable N is used to count NO answers.

```
100    REMARK QUESTIØNNAIRE ANALYSIS PRØGRAM
110    REMARK SET CØUNTING VARIABLES TØ ZERØ
120    LET Y=0
130    LET N=0
200    REMARK READ AND CØUNT ANSWERS
210    READ A
220    IF A=-1 THEN 410
230    IF A=1 THEN 260
240    IF A=2 THEN 280
250    GØTØ 210
260    LET Y=Y+1
270    GØTØ 210
280    LET N=N+1
290    GØTØ 210
400    REMARK PRINT THE RESULTS
410    PRINT
420    PRINT "YES:";Y
430    PRINT " NØ:";N
900    REMARK DATA: 1=YES, 2=NØ, -1=END ØF DATA
910    DATA 1,2,2,2,1,2,1,2,1,2
920    DATA 2,1,1,1,2,1,2,2,2,1
930    DATA 2,2,2,1,2,1,2,2,1,2
940    DATA 1,1,1,1,2,1,2,2,1,1
950    DATA 2,2,2,2,1,1,1,2,1,2,-1
999    END

RUN

YES: 23
 NØ: 27
```

Read through the program carefully. Here are some questions to see if you understand how it works.

(a) When the program is RUN, which section of the program is included in a "loop" that is repeated for each value in the DATA statements?

Lines _____ to _____.

(b) Which statement in the program reads a value corresponding to one vote and assigns it to variable A? _____

(c) Which statement checks the "vote" (values of A) to find out if it is really the end of data flag (−1)? _____

(d) Which two statements in the program determine whether each vote is a YES vote or a NO vote?

_____

_____

(e) Which two statements keep a running tally or count of YES and NO votes when the program is RUN?

_____

_____

(a) Lines 210 to 290

(b) `210 READ A`

(c) `220 IF A=-1 THEN 410`

(d) `230 IF A=1 THEN 260`
`240 IF A=2 THEN 280`

(e) `260 LET Y=Y+1`
`280 LET N=N+1`

25. New questionnaire.

```
DOES YOUR COMPUTER UNDERSTAND YOU?
          1.  YES
          2.  NO
          3.  SOMETIMES
```

Modify the program in frame 24 so that the computer counts the YES, NO, and SOMETIMES answers.

Use the variable Y to count YES answers.
Use the variable N to count NO answers.
Use the variable S to count SOMETIMES answers.

Use the following data:

```
910 DATA 2,1,3,2,3,3,1,3,3,2,1,2,1,2,1,1,3,3,-1
```

Using this DATA statement, the results should be printed as follows:

```
YES:          6
NO:           5
SOMETIMES:    7
```

- -

Our changes:

```
135 LET S=0
245 IF A=3 THEN 300
300 LET S=S+1
310 GO TO 210
420 PRINT "YES:",Y
430 PRINT "NO:",N
440 PRINT "SOMETIMES:",S
```

26. Now let's put the IF-THEN statement to work in a program that tells how long it would take to "double your money" at a given rate of interest.

This program uses a *loop* to calculate interest and to keep a running total of principal plus interest, *until the condition specified in the IF-THEN statement in Line 90 is true.* Since there is no PRINT statement within the GO TO loop, there is no external evidence that the loop has been performed until the IF-THEN condition is true and the computer has "jumped out of" the loop and printed Line 130. Check it out.

```
P  =  Principal
R  =  Rate of Interest
I  =  Interest
Y  =  Year
P1 =  Principal (more on P1 later)
```

```
5    REMARK NUMBER ØF YEARS TØ DØUBLE YØUR MØNEY
10   PRINT "PRINCIPAL";
20   INPUT P
30   PRINT "RATE ØF INTEREST (IN %)";
40   INPUT R
50   LET Y=1
60   LET P1=P
70   LET I=P1*(R/100)
80   LET P1=P1+I
90   IF P1 >= 2*P THEN 120
100  LET Y=Y+1
110  GØTØ 70
120  PRINT
130  PRINT "AT";R;"%, IN";Y;"YEARS YØU WILL HAVE $";P1
999  END

RUN

PRINCIPAL?2000
RATE ØF INTEREST (IN %)?6

AT 6 %, IN 12 YEARS YØU WILL HAVE $ 4024.39
```

Which statements are included in the GO TO loop? Lines _____.
Which line keeps track of the *number of years* it takes to "double your

money?" Line _____ .

Lines 70, 80, 90, 100, 110
Line 100

27. A brief digression regarding Line 60 of the program:

60 LET P1=P

We have used another variable notation which you haven't seen before.

If the computer were limited to the 26 letters of the alphabet for variables, its capacity for handling variables would be limited. You will be introduced to a number of methods for overcoming this obstacle. Here is one way to have more than 26 variables.

A letter of the alphabet with a single digit immediately following it (e.g., A1, A2, M7, etc) is recognized by the computer as distinct from any other variable with or without a digit. The letters A through Z combined with any digit, 0 through 9, give the computer the capacity to deal with 260 (26 letters times 10 digits) variables using this particular notation.

Another use for this new form of variable notation is to point out the relationship between two variables, such as in Line 60. Recall for a moment the "boxes" in the computer where values of variables are stored. Each time through the GO TO loop, the value of P (principal) would be erased and replaced with a new value (Principal plus interest) by Line 80 of the program. However, we need to keep the original value of P for use in the IF-THEN statement in Line 90. So, we invent a new variable P1, and set it equal to P.

60 LET P1=P

Now the value of P is stored in two places; in box P and in box P1. In the program, the value of P is "left untouched" (or at least not changed), and P1 is used to keep the tally of *principal plus interest* for each trip through the loop. Note the use of P1 in Lines 70, 80, 90, and 130.

Understand that we could have used *any* variable instead of P1, for instance

60 LET X=P

and still have a variable holding the original value of P.   Using P1 just helps us keep things straight.   Circle the variables below that are correct BASIC variables.

A   X   X8   BB   4X   N2

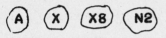

28. Now with that possible source of confusion cleared up, let's delve further into the inner workings of this program.

```
5    REMARK NUMBER ØF YEARS TØ DØUBLE YØUR MØNEY
10   PRINT "PRINCIPAL";
20   INPUT P
30   PRINT "RATE ØF INTEREST (IN %)";
40   INPUT R
50   LET Y=1
60   LET P1=P
70   LET I=P1*(R/100)
80   LET P1=P1+I
90   IF P1 >= 2*P THEN 120
100  LET Y=Y+1
110  GØTØ 70
120  PRINT
130  PRINT "AT";R;"%, IN";Y;"YEARS YØU WILL HAVE $";P1
999  END

RUN

PRINCIPAL?300
RATE ØF INTEREST (IN %)?5

AT 5 %, IN 15 YEARS YØU WILL HAVE $ 623.678
```

(a) Which line checks to see if the principal has doubled by the interest compounding process? Line _____ .

(b) What two values are compared by the IF-THEN statement? _____ .

(a) Line 90

(b) P1, the total of *principal plus interest*, is compared to 2 times P, double the INPUT value of "PRINCIPAL."

SELF-TEST

If you can do the following set of problems, then you are ready to plow right on into Chapter Four, where we unveil some further capabilities of computers, and show you how to get them to do their tricks using BASIC.

1. List the comparisons available for use in the condition part of an IF-THEN statement.

    _____

2. Write the following conditions as IF-THEN statements.

    (a) If the value of X is zero or less, go to Line 80. _____.

    (b) If the value of K divided by 10 is not equal to the value of A times B, then go to Line 150. _____.

    (c) If the value of B1 is equal to or greater than B2, go to Line 350.

    _____

3. Here's a little business problem. Let's say that you sell some items by the case, and also as units. Write yourself a little program that has the following input:

    > Cost per case
    > Number of units per case

    Here's what you want the program to do:

    (a) Compute the per item price based on the per case prices.
    (b) If the per item price is one dollar or under, our item price is marked up 10% over case prices. If the per item price is over a dollar, the markup is only 5%.

    For output, all you want is the amount to put on the price tags of the items sold singly. If possible, check out and debug your program at a terminal before looking at our solution.

4.   Another exercise in program writing. Write a program that will pro-
     duce the RUN shown below, without using READ and DATA state-
     ments.

> **RUN**
>
> ```
> F = 1
> F = 2
> F = 3
> F = 4
> F = 5
> F = 6
> F = 7
> F = 8
> ```

BONUS PROBLEM. Write a program to compute the total pay for people who
are paid based on the number of pieces they produce in a week. The base pay
given to everyone is $200 a week, regardless of how many items are produced.
If a person produces more than a minimum quantity of 300 items, he is paid
the base pay *plus* $1 each for every item produced in excess of the minimum
300. Your program should produce the following RUN.

```
RUN
HOW MANY ITEMS PRODUCED? 150
TOTAL PAY IS $200

HOW MANY ITEMS PRODUCED? 350
TOTAL PAY IS $250

HOW MANY ITEMS PRODUCED? 500
TOTAL PAY IS $400
```

Answers to Self-Test

The frame numbers in parentheses refer to the frames in the chapter where the topic is discussed. You may wish to refer back to these for quick review.

1.   =   (frame 2)
     <
     >
     <=
     >=
     <>

2.   (a) IF X <= 0 THEN 80   (frames 1 to 15)
     (b) IF K/10 <> A*B THEN 150   (frame 27)
     (c) IF B1 >= B2 THEN 350   (frame 28)

3.   There's more than one way to skin a cat; likewise there are many ways to write a price tagging program. Here's one that works. (frame 16)

```
10    REMARK PRICE TAGGING PRØBLEM
20    PRINT "CØST PER CASE";
30    INPUT C
40    PRINT "UNITS PER CASE";
50    INPUT U
60    LET P=C/U
70    IF P>1 THEN 100
80    LET P=P+.1*P
90    GØTØ 110
100   LET P=P+.05*P
110   PRINT "PER ITEM PRICE: $";P
120   PRINT
130   GØTØ 20
999   END

RUN

CØST PER CASE?3.45
UNITS PER CASE?24
PER ITEM PRICE: $ .158125

CØST PER CASE?18.95
UNITS PER CASE?4
PER ITEM PRICE: $ 4.97437

CØST PER CASE?
```

```
4.   10 LET F=1          (frame 21)
     20 IF F>8 THEN 99
     30 PRINT "F =";F
     40 LET F=F+1
     50 GØ TØ 20
     99 END
```

CHAPTER FOUR
FOR-NEXT Loops

In this chapter we introduce the FOR-NEXT loop, the second of the two important computer programming concepts that are sometimes confusing to the beginner. The IF-THEN statement and the FOR-NEXT loop greatly extend the usefulness of the computer as a tool. Close attention to the explanations and problems in this chapter will provide an understanding of the functions of these statements in BASIC and will open a new dimension in your computer programming capability.

When you complete this chapter you will be able to use the FOR and NEXT statements and the STEP clause in FOR statements in writing BASIC programs.

1.   PROGRAM A below is a "counting" program. Line 40 increases the value of F by one each time through the program (that is, every time the computer gets back to the NEXT statement). Line 20 checks the value of F, and sends the computer to the END statement when F is greater than 8.

In PROGRAM A we used a GO TO statement to instruct the computer to "jump" from the last line of the program (before the END statement) back to Line 20 of the program, forming a continuous "loop" that is traced and retraced.

```
PROGRAM A               PROGRAM B

10 LET F=1              10 FØR F=1 TØ 8  ⎫   This is a FOR-
20 IF F>8 THEN 99       20 PRINT "F =";F  ⎬  NEXT loop
30 PRINT "F =";F        30 NEXT F        ⎭
40 LET F=F+1            99 END
50 GØ TØ 20
99 END                  RUN

RUN                     F =  1
                        F =  2
F =  1                  F =  3
F =  2                  F =  4
F =  3                  F =  5
F =  4                  F =  6
F =  5                  F =  7
F =  6                  F =  8
F =  7
F =  8
```

Now, we present (fanfare!) the FOR-NEXT loop (PROGRAM B) to more easily accomplish the same thing. With the FOR and NEXT statement, we tell the computer how many times to go through the loop. Then the computer continues with the rest of the program after the FOR-NEXT loop.

The FOR statement and the NEXT statement appear in separate lines of the program. The FOR statement is the beginning point of the loop and appears first. The NEXT statement is the last statement in the loop. The statements or statement *between* the FOR and NEXT statements are executed in line number order over and over again, with the FOR statement indicating to the computer how many times the loop is to be executed.

You can see from the RUN of PROGRAM B that each time through the loop the value of F automatically increases by one. The computer stopped after going through the loop eight times, because the FOR statement told it to go from 1 to 8.

Fill in the blank: When you have a FOR statement in a program, you must

also have a _____ statement.

––––––––––––––––––––––––––––

    NEXT

2.   As can be seen in the program below, the computer goes on with the rest of the program when it has completed the loop as specified by the FOR statement:

```
10 FØR D=5 TØ 10  ← Note that the loop doesn't have to start with one
20 PRINT "D =";D
30 NEXT D
40 PRINT
50 PRINT "AH-HA! ØUT ØF THE LØØP BECAUSE"
60 PRINT "D =";D;"WHICH EXCEEDS 10."
99 END

RUN

D = 5
D = 6
D = 7
D = 8
D = 9
D = 10


AH-HA! ØUT ØF THE LØØP BECAUSE
D = 11 WHICH EXCEEDS 10.
```

In the preceding program, the FOR-NEXT loop occupies Lines _____ ,

_____ , and _____ .

_ _

Lines 10, 20, and 30

3.   How does the FOR-NEXT loop work? Follow the arrows.

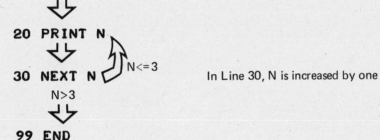

START HERE

10 FØR N = 1 TØ 3   In Line 10, N is set equal to one

20 PRINT N

30 NEXT N   N<=3   In Line 30, N is increased by one

N>3

99 END

As you can see, each time the computer comes to the NEXT N statement, it increases the value of N by one, and checks the new value against the limit for N. In this case, the limit is 3, because the FOR statement reads: FOR N = 1 TO 3. When the value of N is greater than 3, the computer continues on to the next statement after the NEXT statement.

Got that? Let's see.

10 FØR N = 1 TØ 3

means that for the first time through the loop, N = 1.

The second time through, N = N + 1 = 1 + 1 = 2.

The third time through, N = _____ = _____ = _____

_ _

N + 1 = 2 + 1 = 3.

4. Another thing to notice about FOR-NEXT loops is that variables may be used instead of numbers, providing, of course, that the variables have been assigned values earlier in the program. Examples speak louder than words.

```
10 LET A=3
20 LET B=8
30 FØR C=A TØ B
40 PRINT C;
50 NEXT C
99 END
```

In this example, values are assigned by LET statements. Values could also have been assigned by INPUT or READ statements

Semicolon keeps printout on one line (remember the semicolon at the end of the PRINT statements that identified INPUTs?)

```
RUN

   3   4   5   6   7   8
```
← No commas or semicolons printed in the output

Rewrite the FOR statement

```
30 FØR C=A TØ B
```

substituting numerical values for variables A and B. Use the values that were assigned by the program above.

_____

_ _

```
30 FØR C=3 TØ 8
```

5. Play computer and show the RUN for this FOR-NEXT demonstration program.

```
10 LET X=0
20 LET Y=4
30 FØR Z=X TØ Y
40 PRINT Z;
50 NEXT Z
99 END

RUN
```

_____

RUN

0   1   2   3   4

6.   In this program, an INPUT value (Line 50) is used to establish the upper limit of the FOR statement (Line 110), which tells the computer how many times to repeat "X=?"

```
5    REMARK MEAN CALCULATED FRØM INPUT VALUES
10   PRINT "FØR MY NEXT ENCØRE, I WILL CØMPUTE"
20   PRINT "THE MEAN (AVERAGE) ØF A LIST ØF NUMBERS."
30   PRINT
40   PRINT "HØW MANY NUMBERS IN THE LIST";
50   INPUT N
60   PRINT
70   PRINT "EACH TIME I TYPE 'X=?' YØU TYPE IN ØNE"
80   PRINT "NUMBER AND THEN PRESS THE RETURN KEY."
90   PRINT
100  LET T=0
110  FØR K=1 TØ N
120  PRINT "X=";
130  INPUT X
140  LET T=T+X
150  NEXT K
160  LET M=T/N
170  PRINT
180  PRINT "TØTAL =";T
190  PRINT "MEAN  =";M
999  END
```

When the program is RUN, the PRINT statements in Lines 10 – 90 tell the user how to use the program

In the program above, the FOR-NEXT loop occupies Lines _____ .

110, 120, 130, 140, 150

7.   Which line in the FOR-NEXT loop will keep a running tally of the values entered for Line 120? _____

----

140 LET T=T+X

8.   This is a RUN of the preceding program.

RUN

FØR MY NEXT ENCØRE, I WILL CØMPUTE
THE MEAN (AVERAGE) ØF A LIST ØF NUMBERS.

HØW MANY NUMBERS IN THE LIST?5 ← Value entered by user

EACH TIME I TYPE 'X=?' YØU TYPE IN ØNE
NUMBER AND THEN PRESS THE RETURN KEY.

X=?16
X=?46
X=?38   Values entered by user
X=?112
X=?23

TØTAL = 235
MEAN = 47

Show the numerical values in the FOR statement for the above RUN.

110   FØR K=_____ TØ _____

_____

110   FØR K=1 TØ 5   (Value entered for INPUT N was 5)

9.   Here is the beginning of another RUN of the same program.

RUN

FØR MY NEXT ENCØRE, I WILL CØMPUTE
THE MEAN (AVERAGE) ØF A LIST ØF NUMBERS.

HØW MANY NUMBERS IN THE LIST?4 ← Value entered by user

How many times will "X=?" be printed? _____ How many times will
the statements between the FOR-NEXT statements be executed?_____.

_____

4
4

Just to prove it to you, this is the rest of the same RUN.

```
EACH TIME I TYPE 'X=?' YOU TYPE IN ONE
NUMBER AND THEN PRESS THE RETURN KEY.

X=?19
X=?12        Values are entered by user
X=?15
X=?13

TOTAL = 59
MEAN  = 14.75
```

10. Complete the following program to compute the product (P) of N numbers by filling in Lines 100, 110, and 140. Think carefully about the effect of your statements when the program is RUN.

```
5    REMARK PRØDUCT CALCULATED FRØM A LIST ØF NUMBERS
10   PRINT "YØU WANT STILL ANØTHER ENCØRE? I'M FLATTERED."
20   PRINT "I'LL CØMPUTE THE PRØDUCT ØF A LIST ØF NUMBERS."
30   PRINT
40   PRINT "HØW MANY NUMBERS IN THE LIST";
50   INPUT N
60   PRINT
70   PRINT "EACH TIME I TYPE 'X=?' YØU TYPE IN ØNE"
80   PRINT "NUMBER AND THEN PRESS THE RETURN KEY."
90   PRINT

100  _____

110  _____

120  PRINT "X=";
130  INPUT X

140  _____

150  NEXT K
160  PRINT
170  PRINT "PRØDUCT =";P
999  END

RUN


YØU WANT STILL ANØTHER ENCØRE? I'M FLATTERED.
I'LL CØMPUTE THE PRØDUCT ØF A LIST ØF NUMBERS.

HØW MANY NUMBERS IN THE LIST?5

EACH TIME I TYPE 'X=?' YØU TYPE IN ØNE
NUMBER AND THEN PRESS THE RETURN KEY.

X=?7
X=?12
X=?4
X=?3
X=?19

PRØDUCT = 19152
```

```
100 LET P=1            Consider what would happen if P = 0 the first time
110 FØR K=1 TØ N        through the loop
140 LET P=P*X
```

11. Any BASIC expression may be used to set both the initial and the maximum value of a FOR variable, as, for example:

```
10 LET Q=4
20 FOR P=Q TO 2*Q-1
30 PRINT P;
40 NEXT P
99 END

RUN

   4   5   6   7
```

In the following program, fill in the blanks in Line 20 with expressions using the variable Q, so that when the program is RUN, it will produce the printout shown below.

```
10 LET Q=4
20 FOR P=____TO_____
30 PRINT P;
40 NEXT P
99 END

RUN

   2   3   4   5   6   7   8   9   10   11   12
```

————————————————————————

```
20 FOR P=Q/2 TO Q*3
```

or

```
20 FOR P=Q-2 TO Q+8
```

NOTE: If your answer is different and you think it is correct, try it on a computer and see if you get the same RUN that we did.

12.   In the FOR-NEXT loops you have seen so far, the FOR variable takes the first value given in the FOR statement, and keeps that value until the computer comes to the NEXT statement. Then the FOR variable increases its value by one (+1) each time through the loop until it reaches the maximum value allowed by the FOR statement.

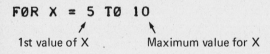

FØR X = 5 TØ 10

1st value of X   Maximum value for X

X = 5, then 6, then 7, then 8, then 9 and then 10

However, you can write a FOR statement that causes the value of the FOR variable to increase by multiples of one, by fractional increments, or to decrease each time through the loop.

10 FØR X=1 TØ 10 STEP 2

Tells the computer to increase
the value of X by 2 every time
through the FOR-NEXT loop
until X is greater than 10

10 FØR Y=3 TØ 6 STEP 1.5

Tells the computer to increase
the value of Y by 1.5 every time
through the FOR-NEXT loop,
until Y is greater than 6

10 FØR Z=10 TØ 5 STEP -1

Note that Z   Tells the computer to decrease
will start at   the value of Z by 1 each time
Z = 10 and   through the FOR-NEXT loop
go to Z = 5   until Z is less than 5

Some demonstration programs will show these capabilities.

```
10 FØR B=1 TØ 10 STEP 2
20 PRINT B;  ◄─────────────
30 NEXT B
40 PRINT
50 PRINT  ◄─────────────────
60 PRINT "LØØP TERMINATES BECAUSE"
70 PRINT "B=";B;", WHICH IS GREATER THAN 10."
99 END
```

This first PRINT statement "bumps" the computer off the line where it is held by the semicolon at the end of Line 20. The second PRINT statement causes the line space before Line 60 is printed.

```
RUN

  1   3   5   7   9


LØØP TERMINATES BECAUSE
B= 11 , WHICH IS GREATER THAN 10.
```

Note that the loop starts with the first value in the FOR statement (1) and increases by increments of 2, until the value of B = 11 exceeds the maximum value allowed (10). At that point, the computer terminates the loop and continues running the rest of the program.

Play computer again, and fill in the RUN for this program.

```
10 LET D=3
20 FØR F=D TØ 4*D STEP D
30 PRINT F;
40 NEXT F
99 END

RUN

_____


- - - - - - - - - - - - - - - - - - - - - -


RUN

  3   6   9   12
```

13. A FOR-NEXT loop may be instructed to perform "backwards," that is, to decrease the value of the FOR variable in any size step, going from a large value to a smaller one. For example:

```
10 FØR J=100 TØ 10 STEP -10
20 PRINT J;
30 NEXT J
99 END

RUN

   100   90   80   70   60   50   40   30   20   10
```

Now you write one where the FOR variable E decreases in steps of 3 from 27 to 18. Show the program and the RUN.

_____

```
10 FØR E=27 TØ 18 STEP -3
20 PRINT E;
30 NEXT E
99 END

RUN

   27   24   21   18
```

14.   One more thing. The steps in a FOR-NEXT loop can be fractional values as in the following example.

```
10 FØR X=5 TØ 7.5 STEP .25
20 PRINT X;
30 NEXT X
99 END

RUN

 5  5.25  5.5  5.75  6  6.25  6.5  6.75  7  7.25  7.5
```

Predict the RUN for this program if we changed Line 10 to read

```
FØR X=5 TØ 7.5 STEP .5
```

RUN

_____

— —

```
RUN

 5  5.5  6  6.5  7  7.5
```

You'll be seeing a lot more FOR-NEXT loops as you continue on in this book.

15.   The FOR-NEXT loop is useful for such things as repeated calculations, counting or keeping tallies, and dealing with cyclical or recurring events.

One such recurring event is the monthly compounding of interest on a savings account or other financial investment.

In the program below, monthly interest (I) is calculated in Line 190 by multiplying the initial amount of money (P for Principal) by the Rate of interest (R).

The rate of interest is converted to a decimal fraction like this:

R = 5 percent = 5/100 = .05.

Since 5 percent is the *yearly* rate of interest, only 1/12 of the calculated amount of interest is added to the principal each *month*.

```
100    REMARK MØNTHLY INTEREST CØMPØUNDING PRØGRAM
110    PRINT "PRINCIPAL";
120    INPUT P
130    PRINT "YEARLY INTEREST RATE (IN %)";
140    INPUT R
150    PRINT "HØW MANY MØNTHS";
155    INPUT M
160    PRINT
170    PRINT "MØNTH","PRINCIPAL","INTEREST","PRIN.+INT."
180    FØR K=1 TØ M
190    LET I=(P*(R/100))/12
200    PRINT K,P,I,P+I
210    LET P=P+I
220    NEXT K
999    END

RUN


PRINCIPAL?200
YEARLY INTEREST RATE (IN %)?5
HØW MANY MØNTHS?6
```

MØNTH	PRINCIPAL	INTEREST	PRIN.+INT.
1	200	.833333	200.833
2	200.833	.836805	201.67
3	201.67	.840292	202.51
4	202.51	.843793	203.354
5	203.354	.847309	204.202
6	204.202	.85084	205.052

(a)   Which lines are included in the FOR-NEXT loop? Lines _____ .

(b)   Which variable keeps track of and is used to print the number corresponding to the month for each line in the table? _____ .

(c)   Line 170 prints the heading for the table. The words used in the heading for the table are separated by commas. In Line 200, the values to be printed under the headings are also separated by commas, so that the spacing of headings and the numbers that go under headings match up. What would happen if the statement that prints the heading were included in the FOR-NEXT loop?

_____

_____

(d)   Which line keeps a running tally of Principal plus Interest? Line _____

_ _

(a)   180, 190, 200, 210, 220
(b)   The FOR variable K
(c)   The heading would be printed every time through the loop, between each line of the table.
(d)   210

NOTE: If you want to brush up on your business math, a useful book would be Locke, BUSINESS MATHEMATICS, John Wiley & Sons, New York, 1972.

16. Below is a modification of the "Worlds's Most Expensive Adding Machine Revisited" program.

```
5    REMARK WØRLD'S MØST EXPENSIVE ADDING MACHINE
10   LET T=0
20   READ N
30   FØR K=1 TØ N
40   READ X
50   LET T=T+X
70   NEXT K
80   PRINT "TØTAL =";T
90   DATA ___ 12, 43, 33, 92, 76.25
99   END
```

There are two READ statements in this program. One is inside the FOR-NEXT loop. Which READ statement is only executed once when the program is RUN?

_____

_ _

20 READ N

17. The statement 20 READ N assigns the first value in the DATA statement to the variable N. N is the number of values to be added by the program. What number should appear in the blank we left in the DATA statement (frame 16)?

_____

_ _

5

18. Show the RUN for the program in frame 16.

RUN

_____

_ _

TØTAL = 256.25

SELF-TEST

Now that you have completed Chapter Four, you have acquired enough understanding of computer programming to be able to learn a lot more by experimenting at a computer terminal. As you look at our demonstration programs, you may see some possibilities that we do not specifically deal with. Build on your knowledge by trying out your own ideas. What if ... ?

And now, find out if you really know how to use FOR-NEXT loops by doing the following problems.

1.   Show what will be printed if we RUN the following program.

```
10    LET S=0
20    FØR K=1 TØ 4
30    LET S=S+K
40    NEXT K
50    PRINT S
99    END
```

2.   Show what will be printed if we RUN the following program.

```
10    LET P=1
20    FØR K=1 TØ 4
30    LET P=P*K
40    NEXT K
50    PRINT P
99    END
```

3.   Examine this program. Which of the three RUNs was produced by the
     program? RUN number _____ .

```
10   LET N=1
20   FØR K=1 TØ N
30   PRINT "*";
40   NEXT K
50   PRINT
60   LET N=N+1
70   IF N>10 THEN 99
80   GØTØ 20
99   END
```

4.   Write a program to print a table of N, N^2 and N^3. Use INPUT state-
     ments to indicate what list of numbers you wish included in the table.
     A RUN should look like this:

```
RUN

FIRST NUMBER? 40
LAST NUMBER? 45

N                N-SQUARED        N-CUBED
40                 1600            64000.
41                 1681            68921.
42                 1764            74088.
43                 1849            79507.
44                 1936            85184.
45                 2025            91125.
```

5.   Show what will be printed if we RUN the following program.

```
10    10    LET S=0
      20    FØR K=1 TØ 7 STEP 2
      30    LET S=S+K
      40    NEXT K
      50    PRINT S
      99    END
```

6.   Help us complete this program to print a table projecting growth rate of a population at sepcified intervals over a given time period (years). The formula for population growth is

$$Q = P(1 + R/100)^N$$

where N is the number of years.

```
100    REMARK REQUEST DATA AND PRINT HEADING
110    PRINT "INITIAL PØPULATIØN";
115    INPUT P
120    PRINT "GRØWTH RATE";
125    INPUT R
130    PRINT "INITIAL VALUE ØF N";
135    INPUT A
140    PRINT "FINAL VALUE ØF N";
145    INPUT B
150    PRINT "STEP SIZE";
155    INPUT H
160    PRINT
170    PRINT " N","PØPULATIØN"
180    PRINT
200    REMARK CØMPUTE AND PRINT TABLE

210    _____

220    _____

230    _____

240    _____

999    END
```

RUN

INITIAL PØPULATIØN?205 ← For U.S.A., 1970 (in millions of people)
GRØWTH RATE?1
INITIAL VALUE ØF N?0
FINAL VALUE ØF N?100
STEP SIZE?10

N	PØPULATIØN	
0	205	Results are expressed in millions
10	226.447	
20	250.139	
30	276.309	
40	305.217	

7. Write a program to compute and print the sum of whole numbers from 1 to N where the value of N is supplied in response to an INPUT statement. For example, a RUN might look like this:

RUN

GIVE ME A WHØLE NUMBER (N) AND I WILL CØMPUTE
AND PRINT THE SUM ØF THE WHØLE NUMBERS FRØM 1 TØ N.

WHAT IS N?3
THE SUM IS 6   (Because 1 + 2 + 3 = 6)

WHAT IS N?5
THE SUM IS 15   (Because 1 + 2 + 3 + 4 + 5 = 15)

WHAT IS N?

BONUS PROBLEM. Write a program to compute and print the product of the positive integers from 1 to N where the value of N is supplied by the user in an INPUT statement. A RUN might look like this:

GIVE ME A POSITIVE INTEGER(N) AND I WILL COMPUTE AND PRINT THE
PRODUCT OF THE POSITIVE INTEGERS FROM 1 TO N

WHAT IS N? 3
THE PRODUCT IS 6   This is called N FACTORIAL

WHAT IS N? 5
THE PRODUCT IS 120

.
.
.

Answers to Self-Test

The frame numbers in parentheses refer to the frames in the chapter where the topic is discussed. You may wish to refer back to these for a quick review.

1. **RUN**
   10   The answer is the *sum* of the values of K defined by the FOR statement (K = 1, 2, 3, and 4)   (frames 1 to 6)

2. **RUN**
   24   The answer is the *product* of the values of K defined by the FOR statement (K = 1, 2, 3, and 4)   (frames 1 to 5 and 10)

3. RUN number 3   The FOR-NEXT loop (Lines 20, 30, 40) causes the computer to print a *row* of N stars. The loop is done for N=1,2,3,...10   (frames 1 to 5 and 17)

4.
```
10   PRINT "FIRST NUMBER";
20   INPUT A
30   PRINT "LAST NUMBER";
40   INPUT B
50   PRINT
60   PRINT " N","N-SQUARED","N-CUBED"
70   FOR N=A TO B
80   PRINT N,N↑2,N↑3
90   NEXT N
99   END          (frame 4)
```

5. **RUN**
   16   Similar to question 1, but this time the values of K defined by the FOR statement are K = 1, 3, 5, and 7   (frames 6 and 12)

6.
```
200   REMARK COMPUTE AND PRINT TABLE
210   FOR N=A TO B STEP H
220   LET Q=P*(1+R/100)↑N
230   PRINT N,Q
240   NEXT N
999   END          (frames 12 and 15)
```

7.
```
10    PRINT "GIVE ME A  WHOLE NUMBER (N) AND I WILL COMPUTE"
20    PRINT "AND PRINT THE SUM OF THE WHOLE NUMBERS FROM 1 TO N."
30    PRINT
40    PRINT "WHAT IS N";
50    INPUT N
55    LET S=0
60    FOR W=1 TO N
70    LET S=S+W
80    NEXT W
90    PRINT "THE SUM IS";S
100   GOTO 30                    (frame 15)
999   END
```

CHAPTER FIVE
Functions

In the first four chapters, you have learned the most used and useful BASIC statements:

PRINT	END	LET	INPUT	READ
DATA	IF-THEN	FOR-NEXT		**GO TO**

In this chapter you will meet another type of BASIC language instruction called *functions*. These handy little things do all sorts of jobs to make the computer programmer's work a little easier. Many computer systems have versions of BASIC that include literally dozens of specialized functions for your use. We have selected several of the more frequently used functions to teach you in this chapter. Having learned how to use these few, you will have no trouble using others should the need arise. We also show you how to incorporate into a computer program functions that you yourself invent.

When you finish Chapter Five, you will be able to write statements in correct BASIC notation using the following functions:

INT( )   TAB( )
SQR( )   DEF FN __ ( )
RND( )

You will also be able to use the following new statements in writing programs:

RANDOM (for some systems)
ON ... GO TO (some computers use GO TO ... OF)

1. You may recall how to compute square roots, or perhaps how to use square root tables and interpolate. With your handy-dandy computer and the *square root function*, you can rest easy and let the electronics do the computations.

```
10   REMARK THE SQUARE ROOT MACHINE
20   PRINT "ENTER A NUMBER AND I WILL CALCULATE"
30   PRINT "THE SQUARE ROOT OF YOUR NUMBER."
40   PRINT
50   PRINT "NUMBER";
60   INPUT N
70   PRINT "THE SQUARE ROOT OF";N;"IS";SQR(N)
80   GOTO 40
99   END
RUN
```

```
ENTER A NUMBER AND I WILL CALCULATE
THE SQUARE ROOT OF YOUR NUMBER.

NUMBER?43
THE SQUARE ROOT OF 43 IS 6.55744

NUMBER?25
THE SQUARE ROOT OF 25 IS 5

NUMBER?
```

The square root function has the following form:

SQR( )

This is where you place the value for which you want the square root

You can take the square root of a number   SQR(25)
or a variable that has been assigned a value   SQR(N)
or an expression   SQR(A↑2+B↑2)

Write a program that will print a table of numbers from 1 to 25 and their square roots. A RUN of such a program follows.

RUN

NUMBER	SQUARE ROOT
1	1
2	1.41421
3	1.73205
4	2
5	2.23607
6	2.44949
7	2.64575
8	2.82843
9	3
10	3.16228

```
10   REMARK SQUARE ROOT TABLE
20   PRINT "NUMBER","SQUARE ROOT"
30   FOR N=1 TO 10
40   PRINT N,SQR(N)
50   NEXT N
99   END
```

2.   It is rather strange to see a "dollars and cents" answer, as in a RUN for the interest compounding program, printed as $600.7442. Fortunately, BASIC has a nifty method for rounding off numbers to convenient decimal places or whole numbers. INT (for "integer part") chops off a number at the decimal point, and drops the decimal fraction part of the number (the part to the right of the decimal point). It functions (if you'll excuse the pun) like this:

```
10 LET A = 600.7442
20 PRINT "A =";A
30 PRINT "CHØPPED A =";INT(A)
99 END
RUN

A = 600.7442
CHØPPED A = 600
```

The value you want chopped (in this case, A) goes into parentheses

Simple, right? As with the SQR( ) function, a value, variable, or expression may be placed in the parentheses.

Write a statement using the INT( ) function for Line 170 of the program to calculate population growth (Chapter Two, frame 36) such that "fractions of a person" are dropped from the answers.

```
170 PRINT "PØPULATIØN AFTER";N;"YEARS IS";Q
```

```
170 PRINT "PØPULATIØN AFTER";N;"YEARS IS";INT(Q)
```

3.   However, when dealing with "dollars and cents" answers, we don't want to lose the cents — that is, the two places *after* the decimal point. So we deal with *that* kind of situation in this way.

Look at the program below line by line, read the explanations and see how and why the value of A changes.

```
5   REMARK STEP BY STEP DEMONSTRATION OF ROUNDING
10    PRINT "NUMBER TO BE ROUNDED";
20    INPUT A
30    PRINT "AFTER LINE 20, A =";A
40    LET A=A*100
50    PRINT "AFTER LINE 40, A =";A
60    LET A=A+.5
70    PRINT "AFTER LINE 60, A =";A
80    LET A=INT(A)
90    PRINT "AFTER LINE 80, A =";A
100   LET A=A/100
110   PRINT "AFTER LINE 100, A =";A
120   PRINT "A IS NOW ROUNDED TO 2 DECIMAL PLACES."
999   END
RUN


NUMBER TO BE ROUNDED?.3333
AFTER LINE 20, A = .3333
AFTER LINE 40, A = 33.33
AFTER LINE 60, A = 33.83
AFTER LINE 80, A = 33
AFTER LINE 100, A = .33
A IS NOW ROUNDED TO 2 DECIMAL PLACES.
```

Look at Line 60, and then the printout for that line.

When rounding off numbers, you have to decide whether to round the last significant digit up one, or leave it the same.

Say you want to round 33.333 to the nearest whole number (no decimal fraction).

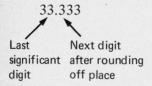

33.333

Last   Next digit
significant   after rounding
digit   off place

If the next digit *after* the rounding off place is 5 *or greater*, then the last significant digit is *increased* by one. If it is *less than 5*, the last significant digit remains the same.

To accomplish the rounding off process in the computer, .5 is added to A *after* it is multiplied by 100. Because the digit after the decimal point is less than .5, adding .5 has no effect on the final result (as you see in Line 100 in our program).

However, examine the results of a RUN of the same program with an input value greater than .5.

```
RUN


NUMBER TØ BE RØUNDED?.6666
AFTER LINE 20, A = .6666
AFTER LINE 40, A = 66.66
AFTER LINE 60, A = 67.16
AFTER LINE 80, A = 67
AFTER LINE 100, A = .67
A IS NØW RØUNDED TØ 2 DECIMAL PLACES.
```

One more example. You fill in the values of A.

```
RUN


NUMBER TØ BE RØUNDED?.2345

AFTER LINE 20, A = _____

AFTER LINE 40, A = _____

AFTER LINE 60, A = _____

AFTER LINE 80, A = _____

AFTER LINE 100, A = _____
A IS NØW RØUNDED TØ 2 DECIMAL PLACES.
```

_____

```
.2345
23.45
23.95
23
.23
```

4. That seems like a lot of work just to round off a number. In fact, Lines 40, 60, 80, and 100 can be combined into one line as in the following program.

```
10    REMARK NUMBER ROUNDING ROUTINE
20    PRINT "NUMBER TO BE ROUNDED";
30    INPUT A
40    LET A1=INT(A*100+.5)/100
50    PRINT A;"ROUNDED TO 2 DECIMAL PLACES =";A1
60    PRINT
70    GOTO 20
99    END
RUN


NUMBER TO BE ROUNDED?.3333
 .3333 ROUNDED TO 2 DECIMAL PLACES = .33

NUMBER TO BE ROUNDED?.6666
 .6666 ROUNDED TO 2 DECIMAL PLACES = .67

NUMBER TO BE ROUNDED?7.825
 7.825 ROUNDED TO 2 DECIMAL PLACES = 7.83

NUMBER TO BE ROUNDED?.314999
 .314999 ROUNDED TO 2 DECIMAL PLACES = .31

NUMBER TO BE ROUNDED?
```

Rewrite Line 40 so that the program rounds numbers to *one* decimal place.

```
40    LET A1 = _____
```

————————————————————————

```
40    LET A1=INT(A*10+.5)/10
```

5.   Look back at the interest compounding program in frame 26, Chapter Three. Write a line to insert in the program that will round off the final balance of principal plus interest just before it is printed by the program. Use an appropriate line number.

_____

Any line number from 121 to 129 inclusive could be used:

```
125 LET P1 = INT(P1*100 + .5)/100
```

6.   Suppose we had put the statement to round off the final balance at Line 115. What other statement would we also have to change?

_____

Line 90 must be changed to direct the computer to Line 115 instead of Line 120.   `90 IF P1 >= 2*P THEN 115`

INT( ) works for negative numbers as well but probably not the way you would expect.

$$INT(-3.5) = -4$$
$$INT(-.2) = -1$$
$$INT(-19.1) = -20$$

7.   *Random numbers* are numbers chosen at random from a given set of
numbers. Many games come with a pair of dice or a spinner or some other
device for generating random numbers. Roll the dice; they come up 8. Move
8 spaces.

In this section you will learn how to use the computer to generate random numbers and use them in various ways. Let's demonstrate. The following program shows the use of the RANDOM statement (Line 20) and the
RND function (Line 40) to print a list of 10 random numbers.

```
10 REM RANDØM NUMBERS    ← REM is shorthand for REMARK.
20 RANDØM                   From now on we will sometimes
30 FØR K=1 TØ 10            use REM, sometimes use REMARK
40 PRINT RND(0),
50 NEXT K
60 PRINT
99 END
RUN

 .5199228   .875198   .5718829   .554516   .1801495
 .09025306  .9201733  .7087619   .9710124  .4472168


RUN

 .9441895   .6401857  .3434087   .2987809  .7020067
 .5230122   .8200131  .2129689   .8976957  .4694544
```

Two RUNs of the program are shown. Are the lists of random numbers in
the two RUNs the same? _____

_____

No

8.   The statement 20 RANDOM causes the computer to produce a *different*
list of random numbers each time the program is run.

The RND function is used to compute numbers that appear to be chosen
at random. On our computer, the RND function is written like this: RND(0)

We will always write the RND function in the above manner with zero
(0) in parentheses following RND. Actually, on our computer, any number
can be used instead of zero without affecting the behavior of the RND
function. On some versions of BASIC, however, what is enclosed in parentheses following RND does make a difference. If you have trouble using
RND(0) on your computer, ask someone to explain how the RND function
works or consult the operating manual or reference manual for the version
of BASIC that you are using.

Examine the list of random numbers in frame 7.

(a)   Is any number less than zero (negative)? _____

(b)   Is any number equal to zero? _____

(c)   Is any number greater than one? _____

(d)   Is any number equal to one? _____

(e)   From the evidence, it appears that random numbers produced by the

RND function are _____ zero and _____one.

No
No
No
No
Greater than
Less than

Important Note: Some versions of BASIC do not include the RANDOM statement. In this case, an error message will be typed if you try to use the program in frame 7. If this happens, simply omit the RANDOM statement (Line 20) and try again. Then, if successive runs produce the same list of random numbers, ask someone how to "RANDOMIZE" your computer.

9.   It's true. Random numbers produced by the RND function *are* greater than zero and less than one. Another way to say it: random numbers produced by the RND function are *between* 0 and 1. Or, in still another way:

$$0 < RND(0) < 1$$

The random numbers produced by the RND function are *uniformly distributed* between 0 and 1. That is, they are "spread evenly" between 0 and 1. A random number is just as likely to be between 0 and .5 as between .5 and 1. In a long list of random numbers, about half of the numbers will be between 0 and .5 and the rest will equal .5 or be between .5 and 1.

(a)   In a long list of random numbers, about _____ of the numbers will be less than .5.

(b)   In a list of 1000 random numbers, about how many will be less than .5?

_____

(c)   In a list of 1000 random numbers about how many will be greater than or equal to .5? _____

_____

half	Remember, we said "about half." The actual proportion may vary with
500	each list of random numbers. For our first real use of the RND function,
500	the important thing is: the probability that RND(0) is between 0 and .5 is about .5

10.   Here is a program to simulate (imitate) flipping a coin. The program prints H for HEADS and T for TAILS.

```
100 REM CØIN FLIPPER
110 RANDØM
120 PRINT "HØW MANY FLIPS";
130 INPUT N
140 PRINT
200 REM FLIP CØIN N TIMES
210 FØR K=1 TØ N
220 IF RND(0)<.5 THEN 250    ← If RND(0) is less than .5, the
230 PRINT "T ";                 computer goes to Line 250 and
240 GØ TØ 260                   prints H for HEADS. Otherwise
250 PRINT "H ";                 it continues with Line 230 and
260 NEXT K                      prints T for TAILS
270 PRINT
999 END
```

```
RUN

HØW MANY FLIPS?100

H T H T H H H T T T H H T T T T T T H T H H T T T T H H H H
H T T T T T T T H T H T T T H T H T H H H H T T T T H T T T
T T T H H H T T H H H H T T H T T T T H T H H T T T H H T H H
H H T T H H T H H T

RUN

HØW MANY FLIPS?100

H H H H T T H H H T T T T T T T H T H T H H H H T T T H T H H H
H T H H H H T H H T T T T H H T T H H T H H H T H H T H H T T T
H H H H T H T T T H T H T T T H T T T H H H T H T T T T T H T H H
T H H T H H H T T H
```

The first RUN produced 43 HEADS and 57 TAILS. The second RUN produced _____ HEADS and _____ TAILS.

52
48

11. Why not let the computer count the number of heads and the number of tails? Modify the program in frame 10 so that the computer counts the number of heads and tails. Use the variable H to keep track of the number of heads and the variable T to keep track of the number of tails. A RUN of the modified program might look like the following:

```
RUN

HØW MANY FLIPS?100

T T H T H T T T T H T H H H H T H T T T T H T T T T T H H H
H H T H H H T T T T H H H T H H H H T T H T T H T H T H H T
H H H H H H T T T T H H H T T T H H T T H H H H H H T H H H
H H T T H T H H H H

   56 HEADS AND 44 TAILS
```

```
203 LET H=0
207 LET T=0
235 LET T=T+1
255 LET H=H+1
270 PRINT
280 PRINT
290 PRINT HJ"HEADS AND"JTJ"TAILS"
```

NOTE: The first "line space" statement 270 PRINT causes the teletype to go to the next line after the end of the H and T printout, in effect counteracting the semicolons at the end of Lines 230 and 250. The second "line space" statement 280 PRINT leaves a line space between the H and T printout and the summary printout. If you are confused about this, try the program on a computer and see the effect of omitting the "line space" statements.

12. Random numbers between 0 and 1 are not always convenient. Sometimes a program requires the use of random digits or random whole numbers or random integers. Below is a RUN in which the computer acts as a teaching machine to teach *one digit* addition to children.

```
RUN

    7 + 2 =?9                    Computer typed: 7 + 2 =?  Student
RIGHT ØN...GØØD WØRK!           typed answer

    3 + 3 =?6
RIGHT ØN...GØØD WØRK!

    9 + 5 =?13
YØU GØØFED. TRY AGAIN.          Student missed this one

    9 + 5 =?14                  Computer repeats problem
RIGHT ØN...GØØD WØRK!           This time the answer is correct

    1 + 4 =?                    New problem ... and so on
```

Undoubtedly, you are anxious to see the program. Patience! Let's build it piece by piece.

First, how do we generate *random digits*?

RND(0) is *between* 0 and 1, but is never 0 or 1. Therefore, 10*RND(0) is

between 0 and _____ .

— —

10

13. In other words, 10*RND(0) is _____ zero and

_____ ten.

— —

Greater than
Less than

14. Below is a program to print random numbers between 0 and 10.

```
10 REM RANDØM NUMBERS BETWEEN 0 AND 10
20 RANDØM
30 FØR K=1 TØ 10
40 PRINT 10*RND(0),
50 NEXT K
60 PRINT
99 END
RUN
```

1.824652	6.206377	.8163955	9.040983	6.898341
.02119429	8.042099	8.061842	5.992168	3.396425

```
RUN
```

6.449042	8.126422	.7171556	1.165139	.5364313
2.732341	1.566163	4.805911	4.739998	5.18679

Now we are going to get tricky and use the INT and RND functions together. First, complete the following:

(a)   INT(1.824652) = _____   (c)   INT(.8163955) = _____

(b)   INT(6.206377) = _____   (d)   INT(9.040983) = _____

_____

    (a)   1
    (b)   6
    (c)   0
    (d)   9

15. Suppose RND(0) = .4739998.

Then 10*RND(0) = _____

and   INT(10*RND(0)) = _____

_____

    4.739998
    4

16.   Now do you see where we are going?

RND(0) is a random number between 0 and 1.
10*RND(0) is a random number between 0 and 10.
INT(10*RND(0)) is a *random digit*.

The following program causes the computer to generate and print random digits, as many as you want.

```
100 REM RANDØM DIGITS
110 RANDØM
120 PRINT "HØW MANY RANDØM DIGITS DØ YØU WANT";
130 INPUT N
140 PRINT
150 FØR K=1 TØ N
160 PRINT INT(10*RND(0));
170 NEXT K
180 PRINT
190 PRINT
200 GØ TØ 120
999 END
RUN

HØW MANY RANDØM DIGITS DØ YØU WANT?100

 0  9  0  9  3  9  7  0  7  0  1  1  7  0  1  9  8  7  7  0
 2  2  1  2  0  6  3  6  9  9  1  8  4  9  6  6  0  9  4  2
 0  8  1  0  9  5  3  3  8  6  0  7  9  0  1  1  6  2  5  2
 5  5  8  6  4  9  5  0  7  8  8  2  6  5  9  3  4  8  9  9
 1  4  0  7  5  7  7  7  8  8  9  2  1  2  5  6  9  3  1  8

HØW MANY RANDØM DIGITS DØ YØU WANT?
```

The first part of the addition drill program follows.

```
100 REM ADDITIØN DRILL PRØGRAM
110 RANDØM

200 REM GENERATE RANDØM NUMBERS A AND B
210 LET A=INT(10*RND(0))
220 LET B=INT(10*RND(0))
```

Now follow this carefully. Lines 210 and 220 produce a random number *between* 0 and 1 (but never 0 or 1), which is multiplied by 10, then chopped by the INT function. Therefore, the value of A will never be greater than

_____ .

_____

9

17.   The value of B will be a random integer between _____ and _____
inclusive.

_ _

0 and 9

18.   The next piece of the program is illustrated below.

```
300 REM PRINT PRØBLEM AND GET ANSWER
310 PRINT
320 PRINT A;"+";B;"=";
330 INPUT C
```

If A is 7 and B is 2, what will Line 320 cause the computer to print?

_ _

7 + 2 = ?

19.   After the student types an answer and presses the RETURN key, the
computer continues.

```
400 REM IS ANSWER CØRRECT?
410 IF C=A+B THEN 600
```

If the student's answer (C) is correct, the computer will go to Line _____.

_ _

600

20. If the student's answer is not correct, the computer next does the following:

```
500 REM ANSWER IS NOT CORRECT
510 PRINT "YOU GOOFED. TRY AGAIN."
520 GO TO 300
```

Assume an incorrect answer. The computer prints YOU GOOFED. TRY AGAIN. and then goes to Line 300. What happens next?

_____

_____

The computer repeats the problem with the same values for A and B.

21. Review the information preceding frame 19. If the student's answer is correct, Line 410 of the program causes the computer to go to Line 600.

```
600 REM ANSWER IS CORRECT
610 PRINT "RIGHT ON...GOOD WORK!"
620 GO TO 200
```

Assume a correct answer. The computer prints RIGHT ON ... GOOD WORK! and then goes to Line 200. What happens next?

_____

_____

Computer generates a new problem (new values for A and B) and prints the new problem.

22.   Below is a listing of the complete ADDITION DRILL PROGRAM.

```
100 REM ADDITION DRILL PROGRAM
110 RANDOM

200 REM GENERATE RANDOM NUMBERS A AND B
210 LET A=INT(10*RND(0))
220 LET B=INT(10*RND(0))

300 REM PRINT PROBLEM AND GET ANSWER
310 PRINT
320 PRINT A;"+";B;"=";
330 INPUT C

400 REM IS ANSWER CORRECT?
410 IF C=A+B THEN 600

500 REM ANSWER IS NOT CORRECT
510 PRINT "YOU GOOFED. TRY AGAIN."
520 GO TO 300

600 REM ANSWER IS CORRECT
610 PRINT "RIGHT ON...GOOD WORK!"
620 GO TO 200

999 END
```

Change Line 210 so that the value of A is a random whole number between 0 and 19, inclusive.

```
210 LET A = _____
```

_____

```
210 LET A = INT(20*RND(0))
```

23.   Change Line 220 so that the value of B is a random whole number between 10 and 19, inclusive.

```
220 LET B = _____
```

```
220 LET B = INT(10*RND(0))+10
```

We made the above changes and ran the modified program.

```
RUN

  6 + 10 =?16
RIGHT ØN...GØØD WØRK!        Remember, a RUN on your
                            computer will probably show
 19 + 12 =?31                different problems
RIGHT ØN...GØØD WØRK!

  8 + 16 =?23
YØU GØØFED. TRY AGAIN.

  8 + 16 =?24
RIGHT ØN...GØØD WØRK!

  7 + 13 =?
```

24.   When the student's answer is correct, the computer always prints: RIGHT ON ... GOOD WORK! In order to relieve the monotony, let's modify the program so that the computer selects at random from three possible replies to a correct answer. The changes are in the portion of the program beginning at Line 600.

```
600 REM ANSWER IS CØRRECT
610 LET R=INT(3*RND(0))+1    Note that we added
620 IF R=1 THEN 630          +1 to our formula
623 IF R=2 THEN 650
627 IF R=3 THEN 670
630 PRINT "RIGHT ØN...GØØD WØRK!"
640 GØ TØ 200
650 PRINT "YØU GØT IT! TRY ANØTHER."
660 GØ TØ 200
670 PRINT "THAT'S VERY GØØD. KEEP IT UP!!!"
680 GØ TØ 200
```

The possible values of R are _____, _____, and _____.

1, 2, and 3   (Not 0, 1, and 2, because we added +1)

---

25. If R is equal to 1, the computer prints _____

_____

RIGHT ØN...GØØD WØRK!

26. If R is equal to 3, the computer prints _____

_____

THAT'S VERY GØØD. KEEP IT UP!!!

27. If R is equal to 2, the computer prints _____

_____

YØU GØT IT! TRY ANØTHER.

28. To our original program (frame 22) we added the changes made in frame 24 and ran the program. The RUN is shown below.

```
RUN

  4 + 5 =?9
RIGHT ØN...GØØD WØRK!

  4 + 4 =?8
THAT'S VERY GØØD. KEEP IT UP!!!

  0 + 9 =?9
RIGHT ØN...GØØD WØRK!

  2 + 0 =?2
THAT'S VERY GØØD. KEEP IT UP!!!

  7 + 5 =?12
RIGHT ØN...GØØD WØRK!

  3 + 9 =?12
YØU GØT IT! TRY ANØTHER.

  6 + 5 =?13
YØU GØØFED. TRY AGAIN.

  6 + 5 =?
```

If the student's answer is incorrect, the computer always prints: YOU
GOOFED. TRY AGAIN. Modify the program in frame 24 so that for an
incorrect response the computer selects randomly one of the following
responses:

YOU GOOFED. TRY AGAIN.
WRONG ANSWER. I'LL GIVE YOU ANOTHER CHANCE.

```
500 REM ANSWER IS NØT CØRRECT

510 LET R = _____

520 IF _____

523 IF _____

530 PRINT _____

540 GØ TØ 300 _____

550 PRINT _____

560 GØ TØ 300 _____
```

— —

```
500 REM ANSWER IS NØT CØRRECT
510 LET R=INT(2*RND(0))+1
520 IF R=1 THEN 530
523 IF R=2 THEN 550
530 PRINT "YØU GØØFED. TRY AGAIN."
540 GØ TØ 300
550 PRINT "WRØNG ANSWER. I'LL GIVE YØU ANØTHER CHANCE."
560 GØ TØ 300
```

29. The three statements

```
620  IF  R=1  THEN  630
623  IF  R=2  THEN  650
627  IF  R=3  THEN  670
```

can be replaced by the single statement

```
620  ØN  R  GØ  TØ  630,650,670  ØR  GØ  TØ  R  ØF 630,650,670
```

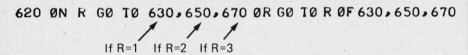

in most versions of BASIC. Using ON R GO TO the program segment in frame 24 can be rewritten as follows:

```
600  REM ANSWER IS CØRRECT
610  LET R=INT(3*RND(0))+1
620  ØN R GØ TØ 630,650,670
630  PRINT "RIGHT ØN...GØØD WØRK!"
640  GØ TØ 200
650  PRINT "YØU GØT IT! TRY ANØTHER."
660  GØ TØ 200
670  PRINT "THAT'S VERY GØØD. KEEP IT UP!!!"
680  GØ TØ 200
```

On most computer systems, the ON ... GO TO variable *must* have a value of 1, 2, or 3 in order to be *true* and to jump the computer to a specified line. Otherwise, like a *false* IF-THEN condition, the statement is passed by and the next statement after the ON ... GO TO is executed. Look at Line 610. What are the possible values of R that this statement can generate?

_____

_____

1, 2, 3

30. Suppose that on a RUN of the program, the random number generated by RND(0) in Line 610 is .3434087. What value will R have? _____
Which line will the computer GO TO from Line 620? _____

_____

R = 2
Line 650

31. The TAB( ) function in BASIC is used in PRINT statements. It's like the TAB on a typewriter, it automatically causes the computer to go to a certain space in a printing line. Here are two programs.

```
10   PRINT "              X                    X"
99   END

RUN
```

Both programs cause X's to be printed in the same place in a line.

```
                 X                    X
```

```
10   PRINT TAB(10);"X";TAB(25);"X"
99   END

RUN
```

```
                 X                    X
```

Recall from Chapter One that up to 72 characters may be printed in one line of output. That is, there are 72 character printing spaces per line. For purposes of using the TAB function, these character spaces are numbered from 0 to 71.

Write a statement using the TAB function, that will cause an X to be printed in the last space in a line.

_____

Write a statement that will cause an X to be printed in the 30th character space *and* in the 41st character space.

_____

_ _

```
20   PRINT TAB(71);"X"
30   PRINT TAB(29);"X";TAB(40);"X"
```

32.   There are some limitations on the values that may appear in a TAB function.

(a)   The value in the parentheses should not be a negative number.

(b)   The value should not exceed 71.

(c)   If the computer is at TAB character space number 55, the terminal printing or display mechanism cannot tab "backwards" to TAB(25); that is, it cannot backspace to TAB character space number 25.

Keeping the above limitations in mind, the value in the parentheses of the TAB function may be:

(d)   a number   **TAB(23)**

(e)   a variable   **TAB(A)**

(f)   an expression   **TAB(W+INT(10*RND(0))**

Which of the following three programs contain TAB instructions that violate one or more of the limitations above? _____

```
PROGRAM A                        PROGRAM C
10   FØR K=1 TØ 12               10   LET M=43
20   PRINT TAB(K);"*"            20   PRINT TAB(2*M);M
30   NEXT K                      99   END
99   END

PROGRAM B
10   READ Y
20   PRINT TAB(Y);Y
30   GØTØ 10
90   DATA 62,39,5,53,11,48
99   END
```

PROGRAM C

33. Show the approximate appearance of a RUN of PROGRAM A in the preceding frame.

RUN

_____

RUN

```
  *
    *
      *
        *
          *
            *
              *
                *
                  *
                    *
```

34. The most common uses for TAB functions are:

(a) for computer art and graphics.

(b) for printing mathematically desired graphs and curves. (For information on programming graphs and mathematical functions, see, for example, Kemeny and Kurtz, BASIC PROGRAMMING (2nd edition), John Wiley & Sons, 1971.)

Note also that the statement

60 PRINT TAB(10);Y;TAB(52);Z

means "print the value of Y at TAB character space 10 and the value of Z at TAB character space 52."

It *does not* mean "print the value of Z, 52 spaces past the print position where Y is printed."

Using READ and DATA statements, as well as the TAB function, write a program that will sort a list of yearly income figures into three categories and columns, using this data.

DATA 3352, 10783, 22852, 19667, 4837, 8956
DATA 9112, 2522, 4890, 6556, 14936

A RUN of your program should look like this:

```
RUN

UNDER $5000          $5000 TO 10000                    OVER $10000
   3352
                                                          10783
                                                          22852
                                                          19667
   4837
                        8956
                        9112
   2522
   4890
                        6556
                                                          14936

OUT OF DATA   IN LINE 20
```

This is our solution. If possible, check yours on a computer if it is
different.

```
5    REM INCOME SORTING PROGRAM
10   PRINT "UNDER $5000";TAB(20);"$5000 TO 10000";
15   PRINT TAB(50);"OVER $10000"
20   READ M
30   IF M<5000 THEN 90
40   IF M<10000 THEN 70
50   PRINT TAB(50);M
60   GOTO 20
70   PRINT TAB(22);M
80   GOTO 20
90   PRINT M
100   GOTO 20
900   DATA 3352,10783,22852,19667,4837,8956
910   DATA 9112,2522,4890,6556,14936
999   END
```

35.   A computer that uses BASIC has a number of functions, such as the INT, SQR, RND, and TAB functions, preprogrammed into it as part of the BASIC computer language itself. However, BASIC also provides a way of making up your *own* functions that will do specialized jobs or calculations, just like the specialized number chopping INT function. These special user-defined functions are invented and written as a statement in a program, then used in the program wherever needed, in the same way you would use the INT or any other function.

It is just a bit tricky, so pay close attention. This is the form of a statement that *defines* a function. In this case, we are defining the number-rounding statement as FunctioN R, or FNR.

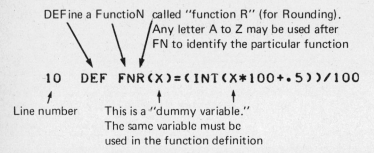

When the defined function is put to use in a program, the variable on which the function is to operate is substituted for the "dummy variable" X.

In the program which follows, the expression used to round a value to two decimal places has been defined as a function (FNR). When we want the value of variable A rounded, that variable is placed in the parentheses following FNR — the "code word" for the number-rounding function. See Line 40.

```
5    REM USING A DEFINED FUNCTIØN TØ RØUND NUMBERS
10   DEF FNR(X)=(INT(X*100+.5))/100
20   PRINT "NUMBER TØ BE RØUNDED";
30   INPUT A
40   PRINT A;"RØUNDED TØ 2 DECIMAL PLACES =";FNR(A)
50   PRINT
60   GØTØ 20
99   END
RUN


NUMBER TØ BE RØUNDED?.333333
 .333333    RØUNDED TØ 2 DECIMAL PLACES = .33

NUMBER TØ BE RØUNDED?.666666
 .666666    RØUNDED TØ 2 DECIMAL PLACES = .67

NUMBER TØ BE RØUNDED?600.744
 600.744    RØUNDED TØ 2 DECIMAL PLACES = 600.74

NUMBER TØ BE RØUNDED?
```

As with other functions, the value that appears in the parentheses of a defined function may be:

(a) _____

(b) _____

(c) _____

    (a)   a number
    (b)   a variable
    (c)   an expression

36. Modify the Fahrenheit to Celsius conversion program found in the Self-Test for Chapter Two, so that a defined function is used to round the temperature to the nearest 1/10 of a degree.

```
DEF FNT(X)=(INT(X*10+.5))/10
```

Note: Many computer systems use a version of BASIC that allows you to define very complex functions using more than one statement in the definition. Consult a reference manual for your computer system to determine how to define multi-statement functions.

SELF-TEST

A word of encouragement: You are learning the functional use of a lot of symbols; don't get discouraged if you haven't been able to write a chess-playing program for your computer system yet. You will learn more about computer capabilities as you learn more of BASIC. Remember, computer programming is a tool to help you and not necessarily an end in itself. Begin considering whether the computer as a tool can have useful applications in those areas of most interest to you, and how you could write appropriate programs.

1.   Write the BASIC notation for the following functions:

   (a)   square root _____

   (b)   integer part _____

   (c)   random number _____

   (d)   carriage tab _____

2.   Write a statement for a program that will define function A as 4 times 3.1416 times R^2. $A = 4\pi R^2$ = surface area of a sphere.

   110 _____

3.   You are a building contractor figuring an estimate on a geodesic dome building (or perhaps you are considering building your own). You need to know about how many square feet of wood or other material will be needed to cover the outside surface of the dome, which is very much like a *half sphere*. You defined a function to calculate the surface area of a whole sphere in the problem preceding in this Self-Test. Use it in your program. Design your program so that it prints a table of surface area and materials cost for enclosing domes with diameters from 12 feet to 40 feet (the radius R is ½ the diameter).
   This is the information the table should provide:

   (a)   the diameter (from 12 feet to 40 feet, at ½-foot intervals).
   (b)   the surface area of the dome, rounded to the nearest square foot.
   (c)   the cost of the surfacing material, at 10 cents per square foot, rounded to the nearest cent.
   (d)   the cost of the surfacing material at 12 cents per square foot, rounded to the nearest cent.
   (e)   the cost of the surfacing material at 15 cents per square foot, rounded to the nearest cent.

(f) the cost of the surfacing material at 20 cents per square foot, rounded to the nearest cent.

Use the TAB function to arrange the columns about the same distance apart across the printout. If you are using a terminal, check the reference manual for your system to see if it has a PRINT USING statement for designing output format. Also, you may need to know whether your system requires 12 or more character spaces to print non-integers, even when rounded off. Isn't computer programming a real challenge?

4. Write a program that will give your little brother, sister, son, or daughter (etc.) practice in multiplication. Design the program so that the user can select one-digit or two-digit multipliers by means of an INPUT statement.

5. Which RUN was produced by this program? _____

```
10   FØR X=1 TØ 8
20   PRINT TAB(X-1);
30   FØR A=1 TØ 8
40   PRINT "*";
50   NEXT A
60   PRINT
70   NEXT X
99   END
```

RUN A   RUN B

```
       *              ********
      ***              ********
     *****              ********
    *******              ********
   ********              ********
  **********              ********
 ************              ********
**************              ********
```

BONUS PROBLEM. Write a program that will produce the other RUN in question 5.

Answers to Self-Test

The frame numbers in parentheses refer to the frames in the chapter where the topic is discussed. You may wish to refer back to these for quick review.

1. (a) SQR( )   (frame 1)
   (b) INT( )   (frame 2)
   (c) RND(0)   (frames 7 and 8)
   (d) TAB( )   (frame 31)

2. **110 DEF FNA(R) = 4*3.1416*R↑2**   (frame 35)

       Dummy variable
       Any variable is okay

3. (frames 31 and 35)

```
100 REM DOME SURFACE AREA AND MATERIALS COST
110 DEF FNA(R)=4*3.1416*R↑2
120 DEF FNR(X)=(INT(X*100+.5))/100
130 PRINT "DIAM.";TAB(10);"SQ.FT.";TAB(20);"$.10/SQFT";
135 PRINT TAB(30);"$.12/SQFT";TAB(40);"$.15/SQFT";
140 PRINT TAB(50);"$.20/SQFT"
150 FOR D=12 TO 40 STEP .5
160 LET A=INT(FNA(D/2)/2)
170 PRINT D;TAB(10);A;TAB(20);FNR(A*.1);TAB(30);
180 PRINT FNR(A*.12);TAB(40);FNR(A*.15);TAB(50);FNR(A*.2)
190 NEXT D
999 END
RUN
```

	SQ.FT.	$.10/SQFT	$.12/SQFT	$.15/SQFT	$.20/SQFT
12	226	22.6	27.12	33.9	45.2
12.5	245	24.5	29.4	36.75	49
13	265	26.5	31.8	39.75	53
13.5	286	28.6	34.32	42.9	57.2
14	307	30.7	36.84	46.05	61.4
14.5	330	33	39.6	49.5	66
15	353	35.3	42.36	52.95	70.6

(We have cut off the rest of the RUN to save space.)

Note: **160 LET A=INT(FNA(D/2)/2)**

   Half the diameter is radius   Half the surface of a sphere is a dome

Note also that we used two PRINT statements to print one line of the table. A semicolon was used at the end of Lines 130 and 170.

4.   (frames 12 to 22)

```
100   REM MULTIPLICATIØN PRACTICE: ØNE ØR TWØ DIGIT
110   PRINT "AFTER THE QUESTIØN MARK, TYPE 1 IF YØU WANT TØ DØ"
120   PRINT "ØNE DIGIT MULTIPLICATIØN (5 TIMES 5 = 25) ØR"
130   PRINT "TYPE 2 IF YØU WANT TØ DØ TWØ DIGIT MULTIPLICATIØN"
140   PRINT "(12 TIMES 20 = 240)."
150   PRINT "1 ØR 2";
160   INPUT M
170   PRINT
180   IF M=1 THEN 210
190   IF M=2 THEN 230
200   GØTØ 110
210   LET X=10
220   GØTØ 240
230   LET X=100
240   LET A=INT(X*RND(0))
250   LET B=INT(X*RND(0))
300   REM PRØBLEM AND STUDENT ANSWER
310   PRINT A;"TIMES";B;"=";
320   INPUT P
330   IF P=A*B THEN 400
340   GØTØ 500
400   REM CØMPUTER RESPØNSE TØ CØRRECT ANSWER
410   PRINT "GØØD SHØW! TRY ANØTHER."
420   PRINT
430   GØTØ 240
500   REM CØMPUTER RESPØNSE TØ INCØRRECT ANSWER
510   PRINT "SØRRY 'BØUT THAT. TRY AGAIN."
520   PRINT
530   GØTØ 300
999   END
RUN


AFTER THE QUESTIØN MARK, TYPE 1 IF YØU WANT TØ DØ
ØNE DIGIT MULTIPLICATIØN (5 TIMES 5 = 25) ØR
TYPE 2 IF YØU WANT TØ DØ TWØ DIGIT MULTIPLICATIØN
(12 TIMES 20 = 240).
1 ØR 2?1

 3    TIMES 1    =?3
GØØD SHØW! TRY ANØTHER.

 7    TIMES 8    =?58
SØRRY 'BØUT THAT. TRY AGAIN.

 7    TIMES 8    =?56
GØØD SHØW! TRY ANØTHER.

 6    TIMES 0    =?0
GØØD SHØW! TRY ANØTHER.

 5    TIMES 8    =?
```

5.   RUN B   (frames 31 to 34)

CHAPTER SIX

Subscripted Variables

In Chapters Six and Seven we will present a useful tool, the *subscripted variable*. In this chapter we will discuss BASIC variables with a *single* subscript, and introduce a new instruction, the DIMension statement.

One of the most common uses for subscripted variables is in representing *arrays* or *matrices* of numbers; in a matrix the numbers are arranged in rows and columns. A matrix with only one row or one column (represented by a single subscripted variable) is also termed a *list* or a *vector*.

Many versions of BASIC contain a special set of instructions called MATrix functions. You will learn to use four of these:

MAT ZERO
MAT PRINT
MAT INPUT
MAT READ

1.   The next concept we will discuss will require your close attention. Take it slowly, and read carefully as we enter the mysterious realm of *subscripted variables*.

Until now, we have used only *simple* BASIC variables. A simple variable consists of a letter (any letter A to Z) or a letter *followed by* a single digit (any digit 0 to 9).

For example, the following are simple variables:

P   R   K   P1   P2

Now we want to introduce a new type of variable, called a subscripted variable.

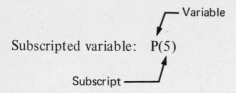

Subscripted variable: P(5)

Say it like this: "P sub 5"

A subscripted variable consists of a letter (any letter A to Z) followed by a subscript *enclosed in parentheses*.

P(3)   is a subscripted variable.
P3   is *not* a subscripted variable.

Which of the following are subscripted variables?   Circle the answer(s).

X(1)   X   X1   C(23)   D

_ _ _ _ _ _ _ _ _ _ _ _ _ _ _ _ _ _ _ _

KNOW THIS: X, X1, and X(1) are three distinct variables. All three can appear in the same program. They may confuse you, but the computer will recognize them as three different variables.

2.   A subscripted variable (like the simple variables we have been using) names a location inside the computer; you can think of it as a box, a place to store a number.

EIGHT SUBSCRIPTED VARIABLES

P(1)

P(2)

P(3)   A set of subscripted variables is also
                called an *array*. This set of subscripted
P(4)   variables is a *one-dimensional array*,
                also know as a list or vector. Later we
P(5)   will discuss two-dimensional arrays

P(6)

P(7)

P(8)

Pretend you are the computer, and LET P(2) = 36. In other words use your pencil or pen and write the number 36 in the box labelled P(2) above. Then LET P(3) = 12 (do it). Now LET P(7) = P(2) + P(3). Check yourself by looking below.

- -

P(1)

P(2)   36

P(3)   12

P(4)

P(5)

P(6)

P(7)   48

P(8)

3.   So what's so wonderful and mysterious about subscripted variables? Here comes the boggler: *Subscripted variables can have variables for subscripts.*

This subscripted variable, Y(J), has a variable for a subscript.

If J = 1	then	Y(J)	is	Y(1)
If J = 2	then	Y(J)	is	Y(2)
If J = 7	then	Y(J)	is	Y(7)

Let us assume that the following values (in the boxes) have been assigned to the corresponding variables. Note that there are both simple and subscripted variables.

Y(1)	4		Z(1)	4.7		A	1
Y(2)	−3		Z(2)	9.2		B	2
Y(3)	5		X(1)	2		C	3
Y(4)	6		X(2)	3		D	4

Write the value of each variable below:

Y(1) = _____   A = _____   Y(A) = _____

Y(2) = _____   B = _____   Y(B) = _____

Y(C) = _____   X(A) = _____   X(B) = _____

Z(A) = _____   Z(B) = _____   Y(D) = _____

4	1	4
−3	2	−3
5	2	3
4.7	9.2	6

4.   So far we have only used single variables as subscripts. However, the subscript of a subscripted variable can be more complex. Here are two examples, still using the variables and values in the boxes in frame 3.

$Y(A + 1) = Y(1 + 1) = Y(2) = -3$

$Y(2*B) = Y(2*2) = Y(4) = 6$

Now you complete these examples. Fill in the value corresponding to the subscripted variable.

$Y(A + 2) =$ _____ $Y(A + 3) =$ _____

$Y(2*A - 1) =$ _____ $Y(D - 3) =$ _____

$Y(A + B) =$ _____ $Y(D - C + A) =$ _____

$Y(B*C - D) =$ _____

----

5   6
4   4
5   -3
-3

5.   So how can subscripted variables contribute to the ease and versatility of programming in BASIC?

One common use of subscripted variables is to store a list of numbers entered via INPUT statements or READ statements. This can be done by use of a FOR-NEXT loop which causes the subscript to increase by one each time a new number is entered. To illustrate, we will turn once again to our old friend, The World's Most Expensive Adding Machine.

```
100 REMARK WØRLD'S MØST EXPENSIVE ADDING MACHINE (AGAIN)
110 PRINT
120 PRINT "HØW MANY NUMBERS";
130 INPUT N
140 PRINT

150 FØR K=1 TØ N          N numbers are entered by the user
160 PRINT "X=";           and stored in X(1) through X(N)
170 INPUT X(K)
180 NEXT K

190 PRINT

200 LET T=0               First T is set to zero.  Then the numbers
210 FØR K=1 TØ N          in X(1) through X(N) are added to T
220 LET T=T+X(K)
230 NEXT K

240 PRINT "THE TØTAL IS";T
999 END

RUN

HØW MANY NUMBERS?5

X=?37
X=?23
X=?46
X=?78
X=?59

THE TØTAL IS 243
```

For the RUN shown, N is 5. Therefore, 5 numbers will be entered by the operator and stored in X(1) through _____ .

X(5)

6.   Suppose the computer is RUNning the program. It has just completed the FOR-NEXT loop in Lines 150 through 180. The numbers entered by the user are now stored as follows.

N	5
X(1)	37
X(2)	23
X(3)	46
X(4)	78
X(5)	59

The computer is ready to proceed with Line 200. Show the value of T after Line 200 has been executed.

T

T   *0*

7.   Next, the computer will do the FOR-NEXT loop in Lines 210 through 230. How many times will Line 220 be done? _____

5, because Line 210 says FOR K = 1 TO N and N is equal to 5.

8.   Line 220 will be done 5 times, first for K = 1 then for K = 2, for K = 3, for K = 4, and finally for K = 5. Let's look at Line 220.

```
220   LET  T=T+X(K)
```

K is used as a subscript

Line 220 tells the computer to add the value of X(K) to the *old* value of T and then assign the result as the *new* value of T.

What is the value of T after Line 220 has been done for K=1? _____

For K=2? _____   For K=3? _____   For K = 4? _____For K=5?_____

37
60
106
184
243

9.   Let's use the World's Most Expensive Adding Machine to compute the sum of whole numbers, 1 through 12.

```
RUN

HØW MANY NUMBERS?12

X=?1
X=?2
X=?3
X=?4
X=?5
X=?6
X=?7
X=?8
X=?9
X=?10
X=?11
SUBSCRIPT ERRØR AT LINE 170
```

Everything seemed to be going all right, but apparently something is wrong. Help! Complete the following analysis. The first 10 numbers we entered (after 'X=?') were stored in X(1) through _____. Then we entered the 11th number which was supposed to be stored in _____ . At this point the computer printed an error message telling us that a *subscript error* had occurred. Apparently our computer doesn't accept subscripts greater than _____.

————————————————————————

X(10)
X(11)
10

10. That's right. The computer does not permit a subscript to be greater than 10, unless we specify otherwise.

If subscripts greater than 10 are to be used, special instructions must be included in the program to reserve additional space. We must tell the computer the *largest* subscript it is to permit in a subscripted variable by using a DIM statement. DIM is short for "dimensions" of an array of subscripted variables.

105 DIM X(100)

Variable for / Maximum subscript
which space   permitted
is being reserved

The above DIM statement specifies a subscripted variable which can have a maximum subscript of _____.

————————————————————————

100

Note. The *mimimum* subscript, or smallest possible subscript, is zero or one, depending on your computer and the version of BASIC you are using. In this book, we will assume that the smallest subscript is one.

11.   Suppose we wanted to specify that the maximum subscript is 50. Write the DIM statement.

105 _____

————————————————————————

   105 DIM X(50)

12.   We will add the DIM statement from frame 10 to the program from frame 5. Below is a LIST and RUN using the 12 numbers that gave us trouble before.

```
LIST

100 REMARK WØRLD'S MØST EXPENSIVE ADDING MACHINE (AGAIN)
105 DIM X(100)
110 PRINT
120 PRINT "HØW MANY NUMBERS";
130 INPUT N
140 PRINT
150 FØR K=1 TØ N
160 PRINT "X=";
170 INPUT X(K)
180 NEXT K
190 PRINT
200 LET T=0
210 FØR K=1 TØ N
220 LET T=T+X(K)
230 NEXT K
240 PRINT "THE TØTAL IS";T
999 END

RUN

HØW MANY NUMBERS?12

X=?1
X=?2
X=?3
X=?4
X=?5
X=?6
X=?7
X=?8
X=?9
X=?10
X=?11
X=?12

THE TØTAL IS 78
```

Now the program can be used to compute the sum of *at most* how many

numbers? _____

_____

100   If 100 numbers are entered they will be stored in X(1) through
       X(100), the limit specified by the DIM statement in Line 105.
       We can, of course, also use the program to compute the sum of
       fewer than 100 numbers

13.   Instead of using an INPUT statement to get values for X(1), X(2), and so on, we can use READ and DATA statements. We'll put the value of N and the values of X(1) through X(N) in a DATA statement, as follows:

DATA 5, 37, 23, 46, 78, 59

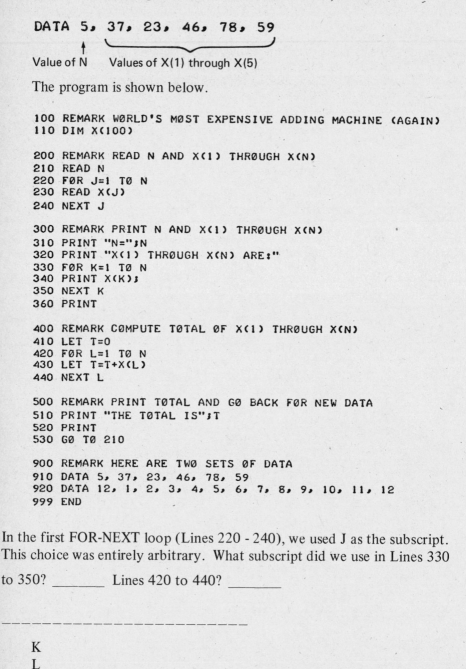

Value of N   Values of X(1) through X(5)

The program is shown below.

```
100 REMARK WØRLD'S MØST EXPENSIVE ADDING MACHINE (AGAIN)
110 DIM X(100)

200 REMARK READ N AND X(1) THRØUGH X(N)
210 READ N
220 FØR J=1 TØ N
230 READ X(J)
240 NEXT J

300 REMARK PRINT N AND X(1) THRØUGH X(N)
310 PRINT "N=";N
320 PRINT "X(1) THRØUGH X(N) ARE:"
330 FØR K=1 TØ N
340 PRINT X(K);
350 NEXT K
360 PRINT

400 REMARK CØMPUTE TØTAL ØF X(1) THRØUGH X(N)
410 LET T=0
420 FØR L=1 TØ N
430 LET T=T+X(L)
440 NEXT L

500 REMARK PRINT TØTAL AND GØ BACK FØR NEW DATA
510 PRINT "THE TØTAL IS";T
520 PRINT
530 GØ TØ 210

900 REMARK HERE ARE TWØ SETS ØF DATA
910 DATA 5, 37, 23, 46, 78, 59
920 DATA 12, 1, 2, 3, 4, 5, 6, 7, 8, 9, 10, 11, 12
999 END
```

In the first FOR-NEXT loop (Lines 220 - 240), we used J as the subscript. This choice was entirely arbitrary. What subscript did we use in Lines 330 to 350? _____ Lines 420 to 440? _____

K
L

14. If we had wanted to, could we have used J in all three places? _____

——————————————————————————————

Yes   These are three separate and distinct FOR-NEXT loops. We
        could have used *any* variable as the subscript except N or T

15. Now the big one. Suppose we RUN the program in frame 13. Show
what the RUN will look like. (Hint: check all the PRINT statements.)

RUN

——————————————————————————————

RUN

N= 5
X(1) THRØUGH X(N) ARE:
 37   23   46   78   59
THE TØTAL IS 243

N= 12
X(1) THRØUGH X(N) ARE:
 1   2   3   4   5   6   7   8   9   10   11   12
THE TØTAL IS 78

ØUT ØF DATA IN LINE 210

16.   Here's a little more practice at doing what a computer does when dealing with subscripted variables, so that you can better understand and use subscripted variables in your programming.

For this segment of a computer program, fill in the boxes, showing the values of D(I) at the affected locations after this FOR-NEXT loop has been run.

```
10    FØR I=1 TØ 3
20    LET D[I]=2*I-1
30    NEXT I
```

D(1) [   ]   D(2) [   ]   D(3) [   ]

----

1   for I = 1, 2*I − 1 = 2*1 − 1 = 2 − 1 = 1
3   for I = 2, 2*I − 1 = 2*2 − 1 = 4 − 1 = 3
5   for I = 3, 2*I − 1 = 2*3 − 1 = 6 − 1 = 5

17.   For the following FOR-NEXT loop, fill in the boxes showing the values in R(1) through R(4) after the loop has been carried out.

```
10    FØR R=1 TØ 4
20    LET R[R]=R↑2
30    NEXT R
```

R(1) [   ]   R(2) [   ]   R(3) [   ]   R(4) [   ]

----

1   for R = 1, R↑2 = 1↑2 = 1
4   for R = 2, R↑2 = 2↑2 = 4
9   for R = 3, R↑2 = 3↑2 = 9
16   for R = 4, R↑2 = 4↑2 = 16

18. Let's do one more of these.

```
10   FØR N=1 TØ 6
20   LET P[N]=2↑N
30   NEXT N
```

P(1) [   ]   P(2) [   ]   P(3) [   ]

P(4) [   ]   P(5) [   ]   P(6) [   ]

- -

```
2     4     8
16    32    64
```

19. Next, assume that numbers are stored in C(1) through C(5), as follows:

C(1) [18   ]   C(2) [34   ]   C(3) [12   ]

C(4) [20   ]   C(5) [17   ]

What will be printed if the following FOR-NEXT loop is carried out?

```
45   FØR A=1 TØ 5
53   PRINT C[A];
67   NEXT A

RUN
```

_____

- -

```
RUN

18   34   12   20   17
```

20. Suppose numbers are stored in C(1) through C(5) as shown in frame 19. What will be printed if the following FOR-NEXT loop is carried out?

```
45   FØR A=5 TØ 1 STEP -1
53   PRINT C[A];
67   NEXT A

RUN

_____
```

```
RUN

17   20   12   34   18      They are printed backwards
```

21. Assume that there is an election approaching and you have conducted a poll among your friends, using the following questionnaire.

> Who will you vote for in the coming election? Circle the number to the left of your choice.
>   1.   Sam Smoothe
>   2.   Gabby Gruff

Let's write a program to count the votes each candidate received in the poll. You have 35 responses to your questionnaire, each response being either a "1" or a "2." First, record the votes in a DATA statement.

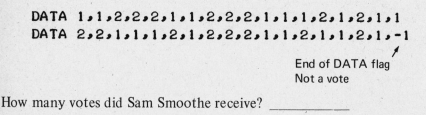

```
DATA 1,1,2,2,2,1,1,2,2,2,1,1,1,2,1,2,1,1
DATA 2,2,1,1,1,2,1,2,2,2,1,1,2,1,1,2,1,-1
```
                                            End of DATA flag
                                            Not a vote

How many votes did Sam Smoothe receive? _____

19

22. How many votes did Gabby Gruff receive? _____ (Do your answers total 35?)

_____

16

23. In order to answer those last two questions, you probably counted the 1's in the DATA statements to find out how many votes Sam Smoothe received. Then you counted the 2's to find out how many votes Gabby Gruff received.

The computer can count votes by using subscripted variables to keep a running total of the 1's and 2's read from the DATA statements. When it comes to the end of data flag (−1) it stops counting and prints the results.

```
100 REMARK VOTE COUNTING PROGRAM
110 DIM C(2)
120 LET C(1)=0
130 LET C(2)=0

200 REMARK READ AND COUNT VOTES
210 READ V
220 IF V=-1 THEN 310
230 LET C(V)=C(V)+1  ◄──────── Crucial vote-counting statement
240 GO TO 210

300 REMARK PRINT RESULTS
310 PRINT "SAM SMOOTHE:";C(1)
320 PRINT "GABBY GRUFF:";C(2)

900 REMARK VOTES FOLLOWED BY FLAG (FLAG = -1)
910 DATA 1,1,2,2,2,1,1,2,2,2,1,1,1,2,1,2,1,1
920 DATA 2,2,1,1,1,2,1,2,2,2,1,1,2,1,1,2,1,-1
999 END

RUN

SAM SMOOTHE: 19
GABBY GRUFF: 16
```

Is the DIM statement really necessary? _____

_____

No, since only C(1) and C(2) are involved, no subscript exceeds 10. However, we feel it is good practice *always* to use a DIM statement.

24. After the computer carries out Lines 120 and 130, what are the values of C(1) and C(2)?

C(1)

C(2)

----

0   These are the *initial* values prior
0   to reading and counting any votes

25. Look again at the crucial vote-counting statement.

```
230 LET C(V)=C(V)+1
```

It is the subscripted variable equivalent of a similar statement which has been used in earlier programs to keep count:

```
LET N=N+1
```

Note how the *variable subscript* of C is used to determine whether either the value of C(1) is increased by one, or the value of C(2) is increased by one. Since V can have only two values, either 1 or 2, Line 230 is actually a double-purpose line. Depending on the value of V, Line 230 is actually equivalent to

```
LET C(1)=C(1)+1  or  LET C(2)=C(2)+1
```

When the preceding program is RUN, what values will the computer have stored for C(1) and C(2) after the *first* vote has been read and processed? (That is, Lines 210 through 230 have been done for the first vote in the first DATA statement.)

C(1)   C(2)

What values will be stored for C(1) after the *second* vote has been read and processed?

C(1) [　　　　]   C(2) [　　　　]

What values will be stored in C(1) and C(2) after the *third* vote has been read and processed?

C(1) [　　　　]   C(2) [　　　　]

- -

C(1) [1   ]   C(2) [0   ]

C(1) [2   ]   C(2) [0   ]

C(1) [2   ]   C(2) [1   ]

26.   Suppose the following poll is conducted.

> Which candidate will you vote for in
> the coming election? Circle the num-
> ber to the left of your choice.
>
>   1. Sam Smoothe
>   2. Gabby Gruff
>   3. No Opinion

The results of this poll are shown below.

2, 2, 2, 1, 2, 1, 1, 2, 1, 1, 3, 1, 3, 2, 1, 3, 2, 1
1, 3, 1, 3, 2, 2, 1, 1, 3, 2, 1, 3, 1, 1, 2, 1, 2, 1, 1

Modify the vote-counting program to process this data. You will have to add
a line to set C(3) to zero, a PRINT statement to print the NO OPINION total,
and, of course, you will have to change the DATA statements for the new
data. And, you will have to change the DIM statement.

––––––––––––––––––––––––––––––

There are the modifications.

```
110 DIM C(3)
140 LET C(3)=0
330 PRINT "NØ ØPINIØN: ";C(3)
910 DATA 2,2,2,1,2,1,1,2,1,1,3,1,3,2,1,3,2,1
920 DATA 1,3,1,3,2,2,1,1,3,2,1,3,1,1,2,1,2,1,1,-1
```

                                          ↑
                            Did you remember this?

27.   Suppose we have a questionnaire with 4 possible answers, or 5 or 6. Instead of writing a separate program for each case, let's write a program to count votes for a questionnaire with N possible answers. The value of N will appear in a DATA statement prior to the actual answers, or votes. For example, the data for the questionnaire in frame 21 would look like this:

```
900 REMARK VØTES FØLLØWED BY FLAG (FLAG = -1)
905 DATA 2
910 DATA 1,1,2,2,2,1,1,2,2,2,1,1,1,2,1,2,1,1
920 DATA 2,2,1,1,1,2,1,2,2,2,1,1,2,1,1,2,1,-1
```

Line 905 is the value of N. In this case, N is 2 and possible votes are 1 or 2. How should the data for the questionnaire in frame 26 be placed in DATA statements?

```
900 REMARK VØTES FØLLØWED BY FLAG (FLAG = -1)

905 DATA _____

910 DATA _____

920 DATA _____
```

```
905 DATA 3
910 DATA 2,2,2,1,2,1,1,2,1,1,3,1,3,2,1,3,2,1
920 DATA 1,3,1,3,2,2,1,1,3,2,1,3,1,1,2,1,2,1,1,-1
```

This time N = 3 (Line 905) and possible votes are 1, 2, or 3.

28.   Your turn. Write a program to read and count votes for a questionnaire with N different possible answers (votes) where N is less than or equal to 20. You will have to do the following things.

(1)   DIMension for the *maximum* subscript for C. Remember, we said N is less than or equal to 20.

(2)   Read the value of N.

(3)   Set C(1) through C(N) to zero. (Use a FOR-NEXT loop.)

(4)   Read and count votes until a flag is read.

(5)   Print the results. Results should be printed like this:

Example: N = 2   Example: N = 3

```
ANSWER #1: 19     ANSWER #1: 18
ANSWER #2: 16     ANSWER #2: 12
                  ANSWER #3: 7
```

Here is the way we did it.

```
100 REMARK VØTE CØUNTING PRØGRAM
110 DIM C(20)                              Maximum subscript = 20
120 READ N
130 FØR K=1 TØ N                           Lines 130-150 set C(1)
140 LET C(K)=0                             through C(N) to zero
150 NEXT K

200 REMARK READ AND CØUNT VØTES
210 READ V                                 This part of the program is
220 IF V=-1 THEN 310                       the same as the program
230 LET C(V)=C(V)+1                        shown in frame 23
240 GØ TØ 210

300 REMARK PRINT RESULTS                   Print totals for answers 1
310 FØR K=1 TØ N                           through N
320 PRINT "ANSWER #";K;":";C(K)
330 NEXT K

900 REMARK VØTES FØLLØWED BY FLAG (FLAG = -1)
905 DATA 2  ← Value of N
910 DATA 1,1,2,2,2,1,1,2,2,2,1,1,1,2,1,2,1,1
920 DATA 2,2,1,1,1,2,1,2,2,2,1,1,2,1,1,2,1,-1
999 END
```
Data from frame 21

The rest of this chapter is about MATrix statements. Most versions of BASIC include these statements, but not all. If your BASIC does not provide the following MATrix statements, you can skip to the Self-Test.

MAT ZER
MAT READ
MAT INPUT
MAT PRINT

NOTE: Most versions of BASIC permit zero subscripts. Therefore, the statement 10 DIM X(5) actually defines a list with 6 members, X(0) through X(5). However, X(0) is not used by MAT operations. All MAT operations assume that lists begin with subscript 1.

29. Here again is the first part of the vote-counting program given as our answer to frame 28.

```
100 REMARK VØTE CØUNTING PRØGRAM
110 DIM C(20)
120 READ N
130 FØR K=1 TØ N
140 LET C(K)=0
150 NEXT K
```

Lines 130 through 150 can be replaced by a *single* MAT statement, as follows.

```
130 MAT C=ZER(N)
```

The above MAT statement tells the computer to set C(1) through C(N) to zero. What is the largest value that N may have? _____

_ _

20, because the DIM statement (Line 110) specifies 20 as the maximum possible subscript for C.

30. Here are some additional examples of how to use the MAT ZER statement. In these examples we will omit line numbers.

Instead of	`LET C(1)=0` `LET C(2)=0`	we write:	`MAT C=ZER(2)`

Instead of	`LET C(1)=0`
	`LET C(2)=0`
	`LET C(3)=0`
		we write:	`MAT C=ZER(3)`

Instead of	`LET C(1)=0`
	`LET C(2)=0`
	`LET C(3)=0`
	`LET C(4)=0`
		you write:	_____

_ _

```
MAT C=ZER(4)
```

31. What's wrong with the following statements?

```
110 DIM D(4)
120 MAT D=ZER(5)
```

_____

_____

_____

_____

- - - - - - - - - - - - - - - - - - - -

Line 120 tells the computer to set D(1) through D(5) to zero. But there can't be a D(5) because the DIM statement (Line 110) says that the maximum possible subscript for D is 4. The computer will print an error message.

32. For each of the following, replace the indicated statements by a MAT ZER statement. (Line numbers are omitted.)

(a)
```
DIM Z(7)
LET Z(1)=0
LET Z(2)=0
LET Z(3)=0
```
replace with: _____

(b)
```
DIM P(99)
FØR J=1 TØ 99
LET P(J)=0
NEXT J
```
replace with: _____

- - - - - - - - - - - - - - - - - - - -

(a) `MAT Z=ZER(3)`

(b) `MAT P=ZER(99)`

33. Next, the MAT PRINT statement. An example is shown.

```
10   DIM A[5]
20   LET A[1]=7
30   LET A[2]=0
40   LET A[3]=4
50   LET A[4]=-3
60   LET A[5]=2.3
70   MAT   PRINT A        Print the values of A(1) through A(5)
99   END
RUN

  7
  0
  4
 -3
  2.3
```

The computer printed the values of A(1), A(2), and _____

_____

   A(3), A(4), A(5)

34. Modify Line 70 so that the computer will print only the values of A(1) through A(3).

```
70 MAT PRINT_____
```

_____

   A(3)

NOTE: You don't need a subscript in a MAT PRINT statement if you wish the entire list to be printed.

35.   Suppose we RUN the modified program. What will be printed?

RUN

RUN

    7   The values of A(1) through A(3) are printed
    0
    4

36.   What will be printed if we RUN the following program?

```
10 DIM B(7)
20 MAT B=ZER(4)
30 MAT PRINT B(4)
99 END
RUN
```

RUN

    0   The values of B(1) through B(4) are printed
    0
    0
    0

37. Write a MAT PRINT statement to replace the following FOR-NEXT
loop. (Line numbers omitted.)

```
FØR K=1 TØ N
PRINT C(K)
NEXT K          Your answer: _____
```

```
MAT PRINT C(N)
```

38. Let's move on to MAT INPUT.

| Instead of | `INPUT X(1),X(2)` |
| we write | `MAT INPUT X(2)` |

| Instead of | `INPUT X(1),X(2),X(3)` |
| we write | `MAT INPUT X(3)` |

Instead of   `INPUT X(1),X(2),X(3),X(4),X(5),X(6),X(7)`

you write   _____

```
MAT INPUT X(7)
```

39. Write a MAT INPUT statement to replace the following FOR-NEXT
loop.

```
FØR J=1 TØ S
INPUT P(S)
NEXT J          Your answer: _____
```

```
MAT INPUT P(S)
```

40. This program is designed to input and print a list.

```
100 REMARK INPUT AND PRINT A LIST
110 DIM X(50)
120 PRINT "HØW MANY NUMBERS";
130 INPUT N
140 PRINT
150 MAT INPUT X(N)
160 PRINT
170 PRINT "HERE ARE YØUR NUMBERS:"
180 MAT PRINT X(N)
999 END

RUN

HØW MANY NUMBERS?5

?7,0,4,-3,2.3        We typed all 5 numbers on the same
                     line with commas between numbers
HERE ARE YØUR NUMBERS:
 7
 0
 4
-3
 2.3
```

Could the numbers be entered as shown in the following RUN? _____

```
RUN

HØW MANY NUMBERS?5

?7
?0
?4             We pressed RETURN after each number
?-3
?2.3

HERE ARE YØUR NUMBERS:
 7
 0
 4
-3
 2.3
```

Yes, the computer will continue typing question marks until N (in this case, N = 5) numbers have been entered.

41.   All right, science fiction fans. Imagine yourself in a school of the
future, called a "Personalized Instructive Learning Environment" and located
in your very own electronically comfort-controlled mini-living space in an
over-population urban center. You have just taken the final examination in
a course entitled "Scientific Managerial Cost Effectiveness Procedures in
Development of Electronic Sensing Devices for Bio-chemical Analysis
Techniques 186.37," usually abbreviated to SMCEPDESDBCAT.

Your P.I.L.E. includes a computer terminal. A program in the computer's memory can score the multiple-guess exam you have just taken.
Here is how you use the program.

```
RUN

YØUR ANSWERS?3,2,4,1,4,2,1,4      Your exam answers
YØUR SCØRE IS 7

YØUR ANSWERS?3
?1
?3
?4          Someone else's answers
?4
?2
?3
?4
YØUR SCØRE IS 5

YØUR ANSWERS?4,3,3
?1,2
?4,3,2
YØUR SCØRE IS 2

YØUR ANSWERS?
```

Now we shall allow you to write the program, under the gentle guidance
of your (by now) beloved authors – Albrecht, Brown, and Finkel.

First write a DIM statement as Line 110 that will allow the program to
compare up to 100 correct answers, to be stored by subscripted variable C,
with an equal number of student answers, to be stored by subscripted
variable A.

```
100 REMARK TEST SCØRING PRØGRAM
110 _____
```

```
100 REMARK TEST SCØRING PRØGRAM
110 DIM C(100),A(100)
```

Note: You can DIMension more than one array in one DIM statement.

42.   The number (N) of items in the exam, and the correct answers for the
exam are stored in DATA statements.

```
900 REMARK VALUE ØF N AND C(1) THRU C(N)
910 DATA 8
920 DATA 3,2,3,1,4,2,1,4
999 END
```

With that information, you can now write two statements to complete this
section of the program: one to assign a value to N, the number of items in
the exam, and the other to assign all the exam answers to subscripted
variable C. Line 220 should be a MAT READ statement. Can you figure out
how it should look?

```
200 REMARK READ CØRRECT ANSWERS INTØ C(1) THRU C(N)

210 _____

220 _____
```

- -

```
200 REMARK READ CØRRECT ANSWERS INTØ C(1) THRU C(N)
210 READ N
220 MAT READ C(N)
```

43.   Look back at the RUN of the program (frame 41); then complete this
section of the program:

```
300 REMARK INPUT STUDENT'S ANSWERS, A(1) THRU A(N)

310 _____

320 _____
```

- -

```
300 REMARK INPUT STUDENT'S ANSWERS, A(1) THRU A(N)
310 PRINT "YØUR ANSWERS";
320 MAT INPUT A(N)
```

44. Now comes the crucial part. Consider what this section of the program must accomplish; then complete the program.

```
400  REMARK CØMPUTE AND PRINT SCØRE
410  LET S=0
420  FØR Q=1 TØ _____
430  IF _____ THEN  450
440  LET S= _____
450  NEXT _____
460  PRINT_____          ← Check the RUN
                                            in frame 41
470  PRINT
480  GØ TØ 300
```

```
400  REMARK CØMPUTE AND PRINT SCØRE
410  LET S=0
420  FØR Q=1 TØ N
430  IF A(Q)<>C(Q) THEN  450
440  LET S=S+1
450  NEXT Q
460  PRINT "YØUR SCØRE IS";S
470  PRINT
480  GØ TØ 300
```

The completed TEST SCORING PROGRAM is shown below.

```
100 REMARK TEST SCORING PROGRAM
110 DIM C(100),A(100)

200 REMARK READ CORRECT ANSWERS INTO C(1) THRU C(N)
210 READ N
220 MAT READ C(N)

300 REMARK INPUT STUDENT'S ANSWERS, A(1) THRU A(N)
310 PRINT "YOUR ANSWERS";
320 MAT INPUT A(N)

400 REMARK COMPUTE AND PRINT SCORE
410 LET S=0
420 FOR Q=1 TO N
430 IF A(Q)<>C(Q) THEN 450
440 LET S=S+1
450 NEXT Q
460 PRINT "YOUR SCORE IS";S
470 PRINT
480 GO TO 300

900 REMARK VALUE OF N AND C(1) THRU C(N)
910 DATA 8
920 DATA 3,2,3,1,4,2,1,4
999 END

RUN

YOUR ANSWERS?3,2,4,1,4,2,1,4
YOUR SCORE IS 7
```

SELF-TEST

So much for science fiction. Back to reality. If you can complete the Self-Test on subscripted variables, you will be ready for the next chapter, which will expand your programming ability to include the use of more complex subscripted variables. Therefore, it is important that you have the information in this chapter well in hand.

1. Which of the following are legal BASIC subscripted variables?

   (a) X   (b) X2   (c) X(2)   (d) 2(X)

   (e) XX(2)   (f) X(K)   (g) X_2 (h) X(I–J)

2. For each of the following subscripted variables, write the subscript separately.

   (a) C(3)   subscript is _____

   (b) Q(A2)   subscript is _____

   (c) S(2*B+C)   subscript is _____

   (d) W(INT(10*RND(0)) + 1)   subscript is _____

3. In 2(d) above, what are the possible values for the subscript of W?

   _____

4. Assume that values have been assigned to variables as shown below. Note that both simple and subscripted variables are shown.

Q	2		A(1)	37
A	3		A(2)	4
A1	1		A(3)	23
			A(4)	19

   Remember, A, A1, and A(1) are distinct variables. Write the value of each variable below.

   (a) A(Q) = _____   (b) A(A) = _____

   (c) A(A1) = _____   (d) A(A(2)) = _____

   (e) A(A(Q)) = _____

5.   What will be printed if we RUN the following program?

```
100 REMARK MYSTERY PROGRAM
110 READ N
120 FOR K=1 TO N
130 READ X(K)
140 NEXT K
150 FOR K=1 TO N
160 IF X(K)<0 THEN 180
170 PRINT X(K);
180 NEXT K
900 REMARK VALUES OF N AND X(1) THRU X(N)
910 DATA 7
920 DATA 23,-44,37,0,-12,-58,87
999 END
```

6.   There is no DIM statement in the preceding program (question 5).
Therefore, what is the largest value of N for which the program can be

used? _____ What would happen if we tried to RUN the
program using the following DATA?

```
910 DATA 12
920 DATA 3,6,-2,0,9,0,7,3,-5,4,-1,7
```

7.   Modify the vote-counting program of frame 23 so that the total votes
(for both candidates) are also printed. The printout might look like
this:

```
RUN

SAM SMOOTHE: 19
GABBY GRUFF: 16

TOTAL VOTES: 35
```

8. Modify the vote-counting program of frame 23 so that the printout is % of total votes, rounded to the nearest *whole number %*.

RUN

SAM SMØØTHE: 54 %
GABBY GRUFF: 46 %

9. Modify the vote-counting program (our answer for frame 28) so that results are printed in % of total votes, rounded to the nearest whole number %.

Example: N = 2

RUN

ANSWER #1: 54 %
ANSWER #2: 46 %

Example: N = 3

RUN

ANSWER #1: 49 %
ANSWER #2: 32 %
ANSWER #3: 19 %

10. Replace each FOR-NEXT loop below with one or more MAT ZERO statements. (Line numbers omitted.)

FOR-NEXT Loop

(a)
```
FØR A=1 TØ Q+1
LET P(A)=0
NEXT A
```

(b)
```
FØR J=1 TØ 5
LET A(J)=0
LET B(J)=0
NEXT J
```

MAT ZERO Statement

_____

_____

_____

11. Show the printout if we RUN each program.

PROGRAM A

```
10   DIM N[5]
20   FOR I=1 TO 5
30   LET N[I]=I
40   NEXT I
50   MAT  PRINT N
99   END
```

PROGRAM B

```
10   DIM W[8]
20   LET W[1]=2
30   FOR P=2 TO 8
40   LET W[P]=2*W[P-1]
50   NEXT P
60   MAT  PRINT W
99   END
```

12. Use a MAT INPUT statement in a program to input a list of numbers, then find and print the largest number in the list. A RUN might look like this:

```
RUN

HOW MANY NUMBERS? 7
WHAT ARE THE NUMBERS? 57,43,75,82,51,68,73
THE LARGEST NUMBER IS 82
```

BONUS PROBLEM. Your boss gives you a series of values that represent sales figures from five (5) geographic sales territories across the United States. Each piece of data is two numbers: The sales territory and the dollar amount of the sales. (eg: DATA 1, 4000, 5, 2500, 3, 6000, 1, 2500.)

Write a program to prepare a report like the one shown below. Be sure to use a single array in your solution.

```
TERRITORY        TOTAL SALES
    1                7500
    2                6000
    3                3200
    4                7200
    5                1800
TOTALS              25700      (the total is a SUPER bonus addition)
```

Answers to Self-Test

The frame numbers in parentheses refer to the frames in the chapter where the topic is discussed. You may wish to refer back to these for quick review.

1. (c), (f), and (h) are legal subscripted variables.   (frame 1)

2. (a) 3   (frame 1)
   (b) A2
   (c) 2*B + C
   (d) INT(10*RND(0)) + 1

3. 1, 2, 3, 4, 5, 6, 7, 8, 9, and 10 are possible values. (frame 1)

4. (a) 4   (b) 23   (frames 2 and 3)
   (c) 37   (d) 19 A(A(2)) = A(4) = 19
   (e) 19 A(A(Q)) = A(A2)) = A(4) = 19

5.   RUN   (frames 7 and 8)

        23   37   0   87

6. 10   (frame 10)
   The computer would print an error message. Our computer printed:

        SUBSCRIPT ERROR AT LINE 130

7. Add the following statements.   (frame 23)

        330 PRINT
        340 PRINT "TOTAL VOTES:";C(1)+C(2)

8. Beginning at Line 310, make these changes.   (Chapter 5, frame 48 and Chapter 6, frame 23)

        310 LET T=C(1)+C(2)
        320 LET S=INT(100*C(1)/T + .5)
        330 LET G=INT(100*C(2)/T + .5)
        340 PRINT "SAM SMOOTHE:";S;"%"
        350 PRINT "GABBY GRUFF:";G;"%"

Someone else did it like this:

```
205 LET T=0
235 LET T=T+1
310 PRINT "SAM SMOOTHE:";INT(100*C(1)/T+.5);"%"
320 PRINT "GABBY GRUFF:";INT(100*C(2)/T+.5);"%"
```

9. Our modifications:

(Chapter 5, frame 4, and chapter 6, frame 28)

```
300  REMARK COMPUTE TOTAL FOR ALL QUESTIONS
310  LET T=0
320  FOR K=1 TO N
330  LET T=T+C[K]
340  NEXT K
400  REMARK CONVERT C(1) THRU C(N) TO %
410  FOR K=1 TO N
420  LET C[K]=INT(100*C[K]/T+.5)
430  NEXT K
500  REMARK PRINT RESULTS
510  FOR K=1 TO N
520  PRINT "ANSWER #";K;":";C[K];"%"
530  NEXT K
```

Super programmer strikes again! He did it like this:

```
205 LET T=0
235 LET T=T+1
320 PRINT "ANSWER #";K;":";INT(100*C(K)/T+.5);"%"
```

10. (a) **MAT P=ZER(Q+1)** (frame 29)

    (b) **MAT A=ZER(5)**
         MAT B=ZER(5)

11. PROGRAM A   PROGRAM B   (frames 33, 34, 35, 36)

    RUN   RUN

PROGRAM A	PROGRAM B
1	2
2	4
3	8
4	16
5	32
	64
	128
	256

12. We did it like this: (frames 39 and 40)

```
100    REMARK PRØGRAM TØ FIND LARGEST NUMBER
110    DIM X[100]
120    PRINT "HØW MANY NUMBERS";
130    INPUT N
140    PRINT "WHAT ARE THE NUMBERS";
150    MAT  INPUT X[N]
160    LET L=X[1]
170    FØR K=2 TØ N
180    IF L >= X[K] THEN 200
190    LET L=X[K]
200    NEXT K
210    PRINT "THE LARGEST NUMBER IS";L
999    END
```

CHAPTER SEVEN
Double Subscripts

In the previous chapter you learned to use

DIM
MAT ZERO
MAT PRINT
MAT INPUT
MAT READ

for writing programs using single-subscripted variables. Now we will extend the use of these BASIC statements to variables with *two* subscripts. Double-subscripted variables are used to represent matrices or arrays of numbers with several columns and rows; a *table* of numbers is an example of such a matrix.

1.   In Chapter Six, we described subscripted variables such as X(7) and T(K). These are *singly-subscripted* variables. That is, each variable has exactly *one* subscript.

X(7)   T(K)

↑   ↑

One subscript   One subscript

In this chapter, we will use *doubly-subscripted* variables, variables that have *two* subscripts.

T(2,3)

↕

Two subscripts. The subscripts
are separated by a comma

T(3) is a subscripted variable with _____ subscript(s).

(How many?)

T(7,5) is a subscripted variable with _____ subscript(s).

(How many?)

_____

1

2

2.   It is convenient to think of doubly-subscripted variables arranged in an *array* of *rows* and *columns*, as shown below.

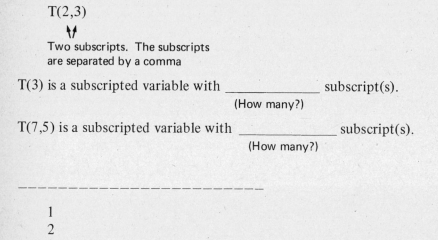

	COLUMN 1	COLUMN 2	COLUMN 3	COLUMN 4
ROW 1	A(1,1)	A(1,2)	A(1,3)	A(1,4)
ROW 2	A(2,1)	A(2,2)	A(2,3)	A(2,4)
ROW 3	A(3,1)	A(3,2)	A(3,3)	A(3,4)

The above array has _____ rows and _____ columns.

_____

3

4

3.   With the arrangement shown in frame 2, we can relate subscripts to particular places (locations, or "boxes" for values) in rows and columns. For example:

$A(2,3)$

Row
Column

$A(1,1)$ is in row 1, column 1. $A(1,2)$ is in row 1, column 2. What subscripted variable is in row 3, column 2? _____

_____

$A(3,2)$

4.   The rectangular arrangement of doubly-subscripted variables shown in frame 2 is called a *table*, or *matrix*, or *two-dimensional array*.

In Chapter Six we described arrays of singly-subscripted variables called *lists*, or *vectors*, or *one-dimensional arrays*.

This is a *list*:	$X(1)$	$X(2)$	$X(3)$
This is a *table*:	$C(1,1)$	$C(1,2)$	$C(1,3)$
	$C(2,1)$	$C(2,2)$	$C(2,3)$
	$C(3,1)$	$C(3,2)$	$C(3,3)$

A list is also called a _____ or a _____ and a table is also called a _____ or a _____ .

_____

vector
one-dimensional array   (one subscript)
matrix
two-dimensional array   (two subscripts)

5.   A doubly-subscripted variable is simply the name of a location in the computer; you can think of it as a box, a place to store a number. Here is a table (matrix, array) of doubly-subscripted variables.

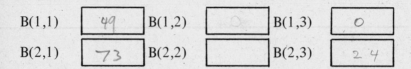

B(1,1) | 49 | B(1,2) | | B(1,3) | 0 |

B(2,1) | 73 | B(2,2) | | B(2,3) | 2 4 |

Pretend you are the computer and **LET B(2,1) = 73**

In other words, take pencil in hand and write the number 73 in the box labelled B(2,1). Then do the following:

```
LET  B(1,3)=0
LET  B(1,1)=49
LET  B(2,3)=B(2,1) - B(1,1)
LET  B(1,2)=2*B(2,1)
LET  B(2,2)=INT(B(2,1)/B(2,3))
```

— —

B(1,1) | 49 | B(1,2) | 146 | B(1,3) | 0 |

B(2,1) | 73 | B(2,2) | 3 | B(2,3) | 24 |

6.   The subscripts can be variables. The subscripted variable P(R,C) has variable subscripts.

If R = 1 and C = 2 then P(R,C) is P(1,2)
If R = 4 and C = 3 then P(R,C) is P(4,3)

If R = 7 and C = 5 then P(R,C) is _____.

— —

P(7,5)

7.   Let's assume that the following values (in the boxes) have been assigned to the corresponding variables. Note that there are both simple and sub-scripted variables.

R	2	T(1,1)	7	T(1,2)	0	T(1,3)	−12
C	3	T(2,1)	9	T(2,2)	5	T(2,3)	8
A	1	T(3,1)	16	T(3,2)	13	T(3,3)	10
B	2						

Write the value of each variable below:

(a)   T(2,3) = _____   (b)   T(1,1) = _____

     R = _____   A = _____

     C = _____   T(A,A) = _____

     T(R,C) = _____   T(B,R) = _____

     T(A,B) = _____   T(R,A) = _____

                                               T(R+1,C−2) = _____

- -

  (a)   8   (b) 7
        2   1
        3   7
        8   5
        0   9
                    16 T(R+1,C−2) = T(2+1,3−2) = T(3,1)

8.   Election time again. (Before starting on this, you may wish to review frames 21 – 26 of Chapter Six.)
     The questionnaire below requires two answers.

> Q1.   Who will you vote for in the coming election? Circle the number to the left of your choice.
>
>   1.   Sam Smoothe
>   2.   Gabby Gruff
>   3.   No Opinion
>
> Q2.   What age group are you in? Circle the number to the left of your age group.
>
>   1.   Under 30
>   2.   30 or over

Since there are two questions, each reply consists of two numbers – the answer to question 1 and the answer to question 2. We will use V to represent the answer to question 1 and A to represent the answer to question 2.

V , A

Answer to question 1   (V for VOTE)
Answer to question 2   (A for AGE GROUP)

The possible values of V are 1, 2, or 3. What are the possible values of A?

_____ or _____

- -

1
2

9.   We sent out some questionnaires. Some typical replies are shown below.

REPLY	MEANING
1,1	one vote for Sam Smoothe, voter is under 30
1,2	one vote for Sam Smoothe, voter 30 or over
3,1	no opinion, voter is under 30

What does the reply 2,2 mean? _____

- -

A vote for Gabby Gruff, voter is 30 or over.

10.   We want to write a program to summarize data for a two-question questionnaire. We will use subscripted variables to count votes as shown below.

	UNDER 30	30 OR OVER
SAM SMOOTHE C(1,1)		C(1,2)
GABBY GRUFF C(2,1)		C(2,2)
NO OPINION C(3,1)		C(3,2)

In other words, C(1,1) will hold the count for Sam Smoothe by people under 30. C(1,2) will hold the total for Sam Smoothe by people 30 or over. C(2,1) will hold the total for _____ by people _____
What subscripted variable will hold the NO OPINION count for people 30 OR OVER? _____

_ _

GABBY GRUFF
UNDER 30
C(3,2)

11. Here are 29 replies to our questionnaire. Remember, each reply is a *pair* of number and represents *one* vote. The first number of each pair is the answer to question 1. The second number of each pair is the answer to question 2.

3,1	2,2	3,2	1,2	1,2	2,1
2,2	1,1	1,2	3,1	3,2	2,2
3,1	2,1	2,2	1,1	1,1	1,2
1,1	2,1	2,1	1,2	2,1	3,1
2,1	3,1	2,1	3,1	2,2	

Write the appropriate count in each box below.

	UNDER 30	30 OR OVER
SAM SMOOTHE	$C(1,1)$ [ ]	$C(1,2)$ [ ]
GABBY GRUFF	$C(2,1)$ [ ]	$C(2,2)$ [ ]
NO OPINION	$C(3,1)$ [ ]	$C(3,2)$ [ ]

- -

$C(1,1)$	4	$C(1,2)$	5
$C(2,1)$	7	$C(2,2)$	5
$C(3,1)$	6	$C(3,2)$	2

12. Naturally, we want the computer to do the counting. Below is the beginning of our program.

```
100   REMARK VØTE CØUNTING...TWØ QUESTIØNS
110   DIM C(3,2)
```

The DIM statement (Line 110) defines an array with at most 3 rows and 2 columns. That is, the DIM statement defines an array of doubly-subscripted variables in which the maximum value of the first subscript is 3 and the maximum value of the second subscript is 2.

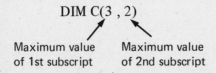

DIM C(3 , 2)

Maximum value   Maximum value
of 1st subscript   of 2nd subscript

Next, we want to set all counts to zero. That is, we want to assign zero to C(1,1), C(1,2), and so on up to C(3,2). *You* complete this part of the program.

```
200   REMARK SET ALL COUNTS TO ZERO
```

Here are three ways to do it!

METHOD 1

```
210   LET C(1,1)=0
220   LET C(1,2)=0
230   LET C(2,1)=0
240   LET C(2,2)=0
250   LET C(3,1)=0
260   LET C(3,2)=0
```

METHOD 2

```
210   FOR K=1 TO 3
220   LET C(K,1)=0
230   LET C(K,2)=0
240   NEXT K
```

METHOD 3

```
210   FOR K=1 TO 3
220   FOR L=1 TO 2
230   LET C(K,L)=0
240   NEXT L
250   NEXT K
```

We will use METHOD 3 because it is easily generalized to arrays of different sizes. We can add more rows by changing Line 210, more columns by changing Line 220. (Of course, we would also have to change the DIM statement)

13. The array is now set up. Next, let's READ and count the votes.

```
300 REMARK READ AND CØUNT VØTES
310 READ V,A
320 IF V=-1 THEN 400
330 LET C(V,A)=C(V,A)+1  ◄—— Crucial vote-counting statement
340 GØ TØ 310
```

Since Line 310 is a READ statement, there must be some DATA statements somewhere. Here they are, featuring the data from frame 11.

```
900 REMARK VØTE AND AGE-GRØUP DATA (FLAG = -1,-1)
910 DATA 3,1, 2,2, 3,2, 1,2, 1,2, 2,1
920 DATA 2,2, 1,1, 1,2, 3,1, 3,2, 2,2
930 DATA 3,1, 2,1, 2,2, 1,1, 1,1, 1,2
940 DATA 1,1, 2,1, 2,1, 1,2, 2,1, 3,1
950 DATA 2,1, 3,1, 2,1, 3,1, 2,2, -1,-1
```

Remember, each reply is a *pair* of numbers representing *one* vote. To emphasize this, we have typed a space after each reply in the DATA statements above.

Why is the flag −1,−1 instead of just −1? _____

_____

_____

If the computer could not find a value for READ variable A (Line 310), it would print a data error message and stop.

14. Only one task remains – print the results! For the data shown in frame 13, the results should look like the following:

```
RUN

CANDIDATE          UNDER 30        30 ØR ØVER

SAM SMØØTHE        4               5
GABBY GRUFF       7               5
NØ ØPINIØN         6               2
```

You do it. Complete the program segment to print the results C(1,1), C(1,2), and so on, as shown above.

```
400 REMARK PRINT THE RESULTS
```

We did it like this:

```
400 REMARK PRINT THE RESULTS
410 PRINT "CANDIDATE","UNDER 30","30 ØR ØVER"
420 PRINT
430 PRINT "SAM SMØØTHE",C(1,1),C(1,2)
440 PRINT "GABBY GRUFF",C(2,1),C(2,2)
450 PRINT "NØ ØPINIØN",C(3,1),C(3,2)
```

15. Here is the complete vote-counting program, except for data.

```
100 REMARK VØTE CØUNTING...TWØ QUESTIØNS
110 DIM C(3,2)
200 REMARK SET ALL CØUNTS TØ ZERØ
210 FØR K=1 TØ 3
220 FØR L=1 TØ 2
230 LET C(K,L)=0
240 NEXT L
250 NEXT K
300 REMARK READ AND CØUNT VØTES
310 READ V,A
320 IF V=-1 THEN 400
330 LET C(V,A)=C(V,A)+1
340 GØ TØ 310
400 REMARK PRINT THE RESULTS
410 PRINT "CANDIDATE","UNDER 30","30 ØR ØVER"
420 PRINT
430 PRINT "SAM SMØØTHE",C(1,1),C(1,2)
440 PRINT "GABBY GRUFF",C(2,1),C(2,2)
450 PRINT "NØ ØPINIØN",C(3,1),C(3,2)
```

NOTE: When you LIST a program your computer may print [ ] instead of ( ). It's all the same so let's not worry about it

Suppose the questionnaire had been the following:

Q1.   Who will you vote for in the coming election? Circle the number to the left of your choice.

    1.   Sam Smoothe

    2.   Gabby Gruff

    3.   No Opinion

Q2.   What is your political affiliation? Circle the number to the left of your answer.

    1.   Democrat

    2.   Republican

    3.   Other

Modify the vote-counting program so that answers are counted as follows:

CANDIDATE	DEMOCRAT	REPUBLICAN	OTHER
SAM SMOOTHE	C(1,1)	C(1,2)	C(1,3)
GABBY GRUFF	C(2,1)	C(2,2)	C(2,3)
NO OPINION	C(3,1)	C(3,2)	C(3,3)

You will have to change Lines 110, 220, 410, 430, 440, and 450.

110 _____

220 _____

410 _____

430 _____

440 _____

450 _____

- -

```
110 DIM C(3,3)
220 FØR L=1 TØ 3
410 PRINT "CANDIDATE","DEMØCRAT","REPUBLICAN","ØTHER"
430 PRINT "SAM SMØØTHE",C(1,1),C(1,2),C(1,3)
440 PRINT "GABBY GRUFF",C(2,1),C(2,2),C(2,3)
450 PRINT "NØ ØPINIØN",C(3,1),C(3,2),C(3,3)
```

Note. Even though we changed the questionnaire, we did *not* have to change the crucial vote-counting statement (line 330).

16. In Chapter Six, we described some of the MAT statements as they are used with lists (one-dimensional arrays). The MAT statements can also be used with tables (two-dimensional arrays). For example, in the program in frame 15 we can replace Lines 210 through 250 with a single MAT ZERO statement.

MAT C=ZER(3,2)

The above MAT statement causes the computer to set up a *zero matrix* with 3 rows and 2 columns, like this:

C(1,1)	0	C(1,2)	0
C(2,1)	0	C(2,2)	0
C(3,1)	0	C(3,2)	0

The statement **MAT Z=ZER(2,5)**

sets up a zero matrix Z with 2 rows and 5 columns.

The statement **MAT T=ZER(25,4)**

sets up a zero matrix T with _____ rows and _____ columns.

- -

    25
    4

17. Write a MAT statement to set up a zero matrix B with 7 rows and 13 columns.

- -

- -

    MAT B=ZER(7,13)

NOTE: MAT ZERO establishes the "working" dimensions of the matrix. However, the program must have an appropriate DIM statement preceding the MAT ZERO statement.

18. Write a MAT statement to set up a zero matrix D with M rows and N columns.

_____

_____

```
MAT D=ZER(M,N)
```

19. This complete program sets up a zero matrix with M rows and N columns and then prints the zero matrix.

```
100 REMARK PROGRAM TO SET UP AND PRINT M BY N ZERO MATRIX
110 DIM T(10,10)
120 PRINT "I WILL SET UP AND PRINT A ZERO MATRIX FOR YOU."
130 PRINT
140 PRINT "HOW MANY ROWS";
150 INPUT M
160 PRINT "HOW MANY COLUMNS";
170 INPUT N
180 PRINT
190 MAT T=ZER(M,N)
200 PRINT "HERE IS YOUR";M;"BY";N;"ZERO MATRIX:"
210 PRINT
220 MAT PRINT T
999 END
```

Line 190 tells the computer to set up a zero matrix called T with M rows and N columns. How does the computer get the values of M and N? _____

_____

_____

The values of M and N are entered by the user at RUN time as directed by Lines 150 and 170.

20. In frame 19, the statement

   220 MAT PRINT T

tells the computer to print a matrix T. The printed matrix will have M rows
and N columns. Why?_____

_____

– –

   The number of rows and columns is originally dimensioned by the DIM
   statement, Line 110. However, Line 190 *redimensions* the matrix to
   have M rows and N columns.

21. Let's look at an actual RUN of the program in frame 19.

```
RUN

I WILL SET UP AND PRINT A ZERØ MATRIX FØR YØU.

HØW MANY RØWS?3
HØW MANY CØLUMNS?4

HERE IS YØUR 3 BY 4 ZERØ MATRIX:

0            0            0            0        Each row is on
                                               a separate line
0            0            0            0

0            0            0            0
```

The computer printed a zero matrix with 3 rows and 4 columns because the
user entered _____ as the value of M and 4 as the value of _____ .

– –

   3
   N

22. Here is another RUN.

```
RUN

I WILL SET UP AND PRINT A ZERØ MATRIX FØR YØU.

HØW MANY RØWS?3
HØW MANY CØLUMNS?8

HERE IS YØUR 3 BY 8 ZERØ MATRIX:

    0         0         0           0           0
    0         0         0

    0         0         0           0           0
    0         0         0

    0         0         0           0           0
    0         0         0
```

The computer prints up to 5 numbers per line. Since each row of this matrix
has _____ numbers, the computer couldn't print the entire row on one
line. Instead, it printed each row on two lines, with _____ numbers on the
first line and _____ numbers on the second line. Note that it *double*
spaces between rows.

_____

8   Since the matrix has 8 columns, each row has 8 numbers

5

3

23. One more RUN.

```
RUN

I WILL SET UP AND PRINT A ZERØ MATRIX FØR YØU.

HØW MANY RØWS?12
HØW MANY CØLUMNS?4

SUBSCRIPT ERRØR AT LINE 190
```

What happened? (If you need a hint, check the program in frame 19.)

_____

_____

_____

- -

The DIM statement in the program defines T as a matrix with *at most* 10 rows and *at most* 10 columns. Therefore, we cannot ask the computer for a matrix with 12 rows. (Unless, of course, we first change the DIM statement.)

24. Let's change the MAT PRINT statement (Line 220, frame 19) as follows:

```
220   MAT PRINT T;     ← Note the semicolon
```

With this change, here is another RUN of the program.

```
RUN

I WILL SET UP AND PRINT A ZERØ MATRIX FØR YØU.

HØW MANY RØWS?3
HØW MANY CØLUMNS?8

HERE IS YØUR 3 BY 8 ZERØ MATRIX:

  0  0  0  0  0  0  0  0

  0  0  0  0  0  0  0  0

  0  0  0  0  0  0  0  0
```

What is the effect of this change? _____

_____

_____

The semicolon following T causes the computer to print numbers more closely together. (Compare with frame 22.)

25. Suppose we RUN the following program:

```
10   DIM A[2,3]
20   FØR R=1 TØ 2
30   FØR C=1 TØ 3
40   LET A[R,C]=R+C
50   NEXT C
60   NEXT R
70   MAT  PRINT A;
99   END
```

What will be printed?

_____

```
RUN

    2    3    4

    3    4    5
```

26. Let's change Line 40 as follows:

    40   LET A(R,C)=R*C

If we now RUN the program, what will be printed?

RUN

    1   2   3

    2   4   6

27. Let's change Line 40 again.

    40   LET A(R,C)=10*R+C

Now, if we RUN the program, what will be printed?

RUN

    11   12   13   The number in a given row and column is 10 times
                            the row number plus the column number. Keep in
    21   22   23   mind the order in which the computer performs
                            the arithmetic functions

28.   We have used MAT ZER and MAT PRINT. Let's take a look at MAT
READ and MAT INPUT. First, MAT INPUT.

```
10    DIM A[2,3]
20    MAT   INPUT A[2,3]
30    PRINT
40    MAT   PRINT A;
99    END
RUN
```

```
?7,0,3   ← Enter ROW 1
??2,4,1  ← Enter ROW 2
```

    7   0   3

    2   4   1

Could we have entered both rows in response to the first question mark as
shown below? _____

   ?7,0,3,2,4,1

_____

Yes, as long as the computer receives 6 ($2 \times 3 = 6$) numbers for the
matrix. We could also enter each number on one line (by pressing
RETURN). The computer would simply keep typing question marks
until all 6 numbers had been entered.

29. Complete the following program to input and print an M by N matrix (M rows, N columns).

```
100    REMARK PRØGRAM TØ INPUT AND PRINT AN M BY N MATRIX
110    DIM A[20,20]
120    PRINT "HØW MANY RØWS";
130    INPUT M
140    PRINT "HØW MANY CØLUMNS";
150    INPUT N
160    PRINT
170    PRINT "PLEASE ENTER YØUR MATRIX."
180    PRINT

190    _____

200    PRINT
210    PRINT "HERE IS YØUR MATRIX:"
220    PRINT

230    _____

999 END
```

```
190    MAT INPUT A(M,N)
230    MAT PRINT A    or    230    MAT PRINT A;
```

30. In a small class of 8 students, each student has taken 4 quizzes. Here are the scores:

	QUIZ 1	QUIZ 2	QUIZ 3	QUIZ 4
Student 1	65	57	71	75
Student 2	80	90	91	88
Student 3	78	82	77	86
Student 4	45	38	44	46
Student 5	83	82	79	85
Student 6	70	68	83	59
Student 7	98	92	100	97
Student 8	85	73	80	77

Let S(I,J) be the score obtained by student I on quiz J. S(5,2) is the score obtained by student _____ on quiz _____. What is the value of S(5,2)? _____

_____

   5
  —2
   82

31. Another class might have 30 students and 5 quizzes per student. Still another class might have 23 students and 7 quizzes per student, and so on. Let's begin a program to read a matrix of scores for N students and Q quizzes per student.

```
100   REMARK QUIZ-SCØRE PRØGRAM
110   DIM S[50,10]
```

The DIM statement permits up to _____ students and up to _____ quizzes.

_____

   50
   10

32. Next, we want to read the values of N and Q for a particular set of scores — in this case, the scores shown in frame 30. For this set of scores the value of N (number of students) is _____ and the value of Q (number of quizzes) is _____ .

_____

   8
   4

33. We will put the values of N and Q and the scores in DATA statements. Now the program looks like this.

```
100    REMARK QUIZ-SCORE PROGRAM
110    DIM S[50,10]

900 REMARK VALUES OF N AND Q FOLLOWED BY SCORES
905 DATA 8,4  ◄──────── Values of N,Q
911 DATA 65,57,71,75 ⎫
912 DATA 80,90,91,88 ⎪
913 DATA 78,82,77,86 ⎬ N by Q array of quiz
914 DATA 45,38,44,46 ⎪ scores from frame 30
915 DATA 83,82,79,85 ⎬
916 DATA 70,68,83,59 ⎪
917 DATA 98,92,100,97 ⎪
918 DATA 85,73,80,77 ⎭
999 END  ◄──────── We also added an END statement
```

Your turn. Complete Line 120, below, to READ the values of N and Q.

120 _____

_____

120 READ N,Q   (That's all there is to it!)

34. The values of N and Q read by Line 120 (in frame 33) will be read from which DATA statement? Line _____.

_____

905

35. Next, let's read the N by Q array of scores.

130 MAT READ S(N,Q)

This MAT READ statement tells the computer to read an N by Q array.

That is, it tells the computer to read a matrix with _____ rows and _____ columns.

_____

N   (Remember, the values of N and Q are read by Line 120.)
Q

36. The numerical values read by Line 130 are stored in the DATA statements, Lines _____ through _____.

_____

911
918

37. Now that we have the matrix in the computer, what shall we do with it? One thing someone might want is the average for each student. Let's do it, beginning at Line 200.

```
200 REMARK COMPUTE AND PRINT AVERAGES FOR ALL STUDENTS
210 PRINT "STUDENT #","AVERAGE"
220 FOR I=1 TO N
230 LET T=0
240 FOR J=1 TO Q        Compute total of all
250 LET T=T+S(I,J)      scores for student
260 NEXT J
270 LET A=T/Q      ◄——— Compute average for student I
280 PRINT I,A      ◄——— Print student number and average
290 NEXT I
```

Lines 230 through 280 are done for each student. That is, for $I = 1$, then $I = 2$, and so on up to $I = N$. For $I = 1$, what is the value of T computed by Lines 230 through 260? $T =$ _____ .

_____

268   This is the sum of the 4 scores for student 1. Remember, $Q = 4$. Therefore, Line 250 will be done for $J = 1$, $J = 2$, $J = 3$ and $J = 4$.

38. For $I = 1$, what is the value of A computed by Line 270?
$A = T/Q =$ _____.

_____

67   ($A = T/Q = 268/4 = 67$)

39. Here is the complete program and a RUN.

```
100 REMARK QUIZ SCORE PROGRAM
110 DIM S(50,10)
120 READ N,Q
130 MAT READ S(N,Q)
200 REMARK COMPUTE AND PRINT AVERAGES FOR ALL STUDENTS
210 PRINT "STUDENT #","AVERAGE"
220 FOR I=1 TO N
230 LET T=0
240 FOR J=1 TO Q
250 LET T=T+S(I,J)
260 NEXT J
270 LET A=T/Q
280 PRINT I,A
290 NEXT I

900 REMARK VALUES OF N AND Q FOLLOWED BY SCORES
905 DATA 8,4
911 DATA 65,57,71,75
912 DATA 80,90,91,88
913 DATA 78,82,77,86
914 DATA 45,38,44,46
915 DATA 83,82,79,85
916 DATA 70,68,83,59
917 DATA 98,92,100,97
918 DATA 85,73,80,77
999 END
RUN
```

STUDENT #	AVERAGE
1	67
2	87.25
3	80.75
4	43.25
5	82.25
6	70
7	96.75
8	78.75

Your turn. Beginning with Line 300 write a program segment to compute and print the average SCORE for each quiz. For the data used in the program the results might look like this:

```
RUN
```

QUIZ #	AVERAGE
1	75.5
2	72.75
3	78.125
4	76.625

Your program segment:

_____

```
300 REMARK COMPUTE AND PRINT AVERAGES OF ALL QUIZZES
310 PRINT "QUIZ #","AVERAGE"
320 FOR J=1 TO Q
330 LET T=0
340 FOR I=1 TO N
350 LET T=T+S(I,J)
360 NEXT I
370 LET A=T/N
380 PRINT J,A
390 NEXT J
```

40. Just suppose a bunch of students take a multiple-guess quiz, 10 questions with 4 possible answers per question. We want to know how many students gave answer number 1 to question number 1, how many gave answer number 2 to question number 1 and so on.

Here are the answers given by 7 students. Each set of answers is in a DATA statement. The last DATA statement is a "fictitious student" and really means "end of data."

```
911  DATA  2,3,1,1,1,2,4,3,4,1        In each line of data, the first
912  DATA  2,3,2,4,1,2,4,2,1,1        number is the answer to ques-
913  DATA  2,3,3,1,1,4,3,3,4,1        tion 1, the second number is
914  DATA  3,2,4,1,1,2,3,3,4,1        the answer to question 2, and
915  DATA  2,3,4,1,1,3,4,3,4,1        so on
916  DATA  2,1,2,3,1,2,4,3,4,2
917  DATA  3,4,1,1,1,4,3,1,4,2
918  DATA  -1,0,0,0,0,0,0,0,0,0       "Fictitious student"
```

Student 1 (Line 911) gave answer 1 to question 3.

Student 5 (Line 915) gave answer _____ to question 9.

Student 7 (Line 917) gave answer _____ to question 1.

    4
    3

41. Complete the following table showing the number of students giving each answer (1, 2, 3, 4) to questions 1, 2, and 3.

	ANSWER 1	ANSWER 2	ANSWER 3	ANSWER 4
QUESTION 1	0	5	2	0
QUESTION 2	1	1	_____	_____
QUESTION 3	_____	_____	_____	_____

----

          4 1
   2   2   1 2

42. In frame 41, with your help, we have shown how the seven students answered the first 3 questions. The totals look like a 3 by 4 matrix. If we had continued for all 10 questions the totals would have looked like a

_____ by 4 matrix.

.10

43. So inside the computer, let's define a matrix T with 10 rows and 4 columns to hold the totals. Complete the following DIM statement.

```
100 REMARK QUIZ ANALYSIS PRØGRAM

110 DIM _____
```

T(10,4)

44. For each student there are 10 answers. Let's define a *list* of answers A(1) through A(10). Complete the following DIM statement.

```
120 DIM _____
```

A(10)

45. But we can save space by *combining* the two DIM statements into *one* DIM statement.

```
110 DIM T(10,4),A(10)
```

The above DIM statement defines a _____ called T with at most 10 rows and 4 columns and a _____ called A with at most 10 members.

_____

matrix (or table or two-dimensional array)
list (or vector or one-dimensional array)

Note that a comma is used to separate T(10,3) and A(10).

46. Here is the beginning of a program to read the students' answers and compute the totals matrix.

```
100 REMARK QUIZ ANALYSIS PRØGRAM
110 DIM T(10,4),A(10)
```

Next, we want to initialize the totals matrix. That is, we want it to be a *zero matrix*. You do it.

```
120 REMARK SET ALL TØTALS TØ ZERØ
130 _____
```

_____

```
MAT T=ZER(10,4)
```

47. Write a MAT statement to read the *list* A of answers for one student.

```
140 REMARK READ ØNE SET ØF ANSWERS
150 _____
```

_____

```
MAT READ A(10)
```

48. Now, is this a real student or a fictitious student? Recall that a fictitious student signals end of data. If this is the case we want to print the answers, beginning with Line 300. Complete the IF statement.

```
160 REMARK CHECK FØR END ØF DATA

170 IF _____ THEN 300
```

———————————————————

```
A(1)=-1
```

49. If the data are for a real student, we want to update the running tally in the T matrix. We did it this way.

```
180 REMARK UPDATE THE TØTALS MATRIX
190 FØR Q=1 TØ 10
200 LET T(Q,A(Q))=T(Q,A(Q))+1
210 NEXT Q
```

Here are the answers for one student. These are the values of A(1) through A(10).

2, 3, 1, 1, 1, 2, 4, 3, 4, 1

Suppose Q = 1. Then A(Q) = _____ and T(Q,A(Q)) is T(_____, _____).

———————————————————

```
2
T(1,2)    (Since Q = 1 and A(Q) = 2)
```

50. In the above case (frame 49) what happens when the computer obeys Line 200? _____

———————————————————

The total in T(1,2) is increased by one. (It's just like counting votes!)

51. Since Line 200 is in a FOR-NEXT loop, it will be done for each value of Q specified by the FOR statement. That is, it will be done for A = 1, 2, 3, 4, 5, 6, 7, 8, 9, and 10. When Q = 10, which element of the T matrix is increased by one? T(_____ , _____).

————————————————————————

T(10,A(10)) or T(10,1) for the data in frame 49.

52. Let's move on. After tallying the answers for one student, we want the computer to return to Line 140 and read another set of answers. (See frame 47.)

```
220 REMARK GØ BACK FØR ANØTHER SET ØF ANSWERS
230 GØ TØ 140
```

Then the IF statement (frame 48) is encountered again. The IF statement causes the computer to go to Line 300 if a fictitious student has been read. In that case, we want to print the results and STOP.

```
300 REMARK PRINT THE TØTALS MATRIX
310 _____
320 STØP
```

————————————————————————

```
310 MAT PRINT T   or   310 MAT PRINT T;
```

Now put it all together. Ours looks like this.

```
100    REMARK QUIZ ANALYSIS PRØGRAM
110    DIM T[10,4],A[10]
120    REMARK SET ALL TØTALS TØ ZERØ
130    MAT T=ZER[10,4]
140    REMARK READ ØNE SET ØF ANSWERS
150    MAT   READ A[10]
160    REMARK CHECK FØR END ØF DATA
170    IF A[1]=-1 THEN 300
180    REMARK UPDATE THE TØTALS MATRIX
190    FØR Q=1 TØ 10
200    LET T[Q,A[Q]]=T[Q,A[Q]]+1
210    NEXT Q
220    REMARK GØ BACK FØR ANØTHER SET ØF ANSWERS
230    GØTØ 140
300    REMARK PRINT THE TØTALS MATRIX
310    MAT   PRINT T
320    STØP
900    REMARK STUDENTS' ANSWERS
911    DATA 2,3,1,1,1,2,4,3,4,1
912    DATA 2,3,2,4,1,2,4,2,1,1
913    DATA 2,3,3,1,1,4,3,3,4,1
914    DATA 3,2,4,1,1,2,3,3,4,1
915    DATA 2,3,4,1,1,3,4,3,4,1
916    DATA 2,1,2,3,1,2,4,3,4,2
917    DATA 3,4,1,1,1,4,3,1,4,2
918    DATA -1,0,0,0,0,0,0,0,0,0
999    END
RUN
```

0	5	2	0
1	1	4	1
2	2	1	2
5	0	1	1
7	0	0	0
0	4	1	2
0	0	3	4
1	1	5	0
1	0	0	6
5	2	0	0

SELF-TEST

Good for you! You have reached the Chapter Seven Self-Test. These problems will help you review the BASIC instructions you have learned for dealing with arrays of numbers, using variables with double subscripts.

1. Which of the following are legal BASIC double-subscripted variables?

    (a) X(2 + 2)   (b) X(5,5)   (c) X1(100,100)

    (d) X(A+B,C)   (e) X(X(1,2), (X(2,1))   (f) X(A,A)

    Questions 2 through 7 refer to the following array, A.

	COLUMN 1	COLUMN 2
ROW 1	1	2
ROW 2	3	4
ROW 3	5	6

2. What are the dimensions of A? _____ , _____

3. Write a DIMension statement for A, using Line number 100.

    100 _____

4. What variable locates the "box" in row 3, column 2 of A? _____

5. What is the value of:

    (a) A(1,1) _____   (b) A(3,1) _____

6. Let X = 3, Y = 2. What is the value of:

    (a) A(X,Y) _____   (b) A(X−1, Y−1) _____

7. What is the value of A(A(1,2), A(2,1) − 1)? _____

8. Write a program which uses two FOR-NEXT loops to fill a 10 by 10 matrix (M) with zeros.

9. Write another program to fill M, a 10 by 10 matrix, with zeros. This time, use a MAT ZERO instruction instead of the FOR-NEXT loops.

10. Write a program using MAT READ to fill a 4 by 4 matrix C with 1's. MAT PRINT the result. A sample RUN might look like:

```
RUN


 1        1        1        1

 1        1        1        1

 1        1        1        1

 1        1        1        1
```

11. Now write another program to fill matrix C (4 by 4) with 1's (or anything you want) using MAT INPUT. Print the result.

BONUS PROBLEM. Certain teachers in your school are complaining of grade deterioration, meaning that some teachers are giving too many A and B grades and are generally not grading hard enough. You are asked to write a computer program to prove or disprove this theory. While you are at it, the local chapter of a Women's group has asked you to prove that women are being discriminated against in grading, receiving poorer grades than men, especially in math and computer science.

The school Registrar provides you with the data you need in DATA statements as follows: DATA 1, 2 2, 4 2, 2 etc. Where the first item indicates sex (1=male, 2=female) and the second item indicates the letter grade (1=A, 2=B, 3=C, 4=D, 5=F). You are essentially counting votes. Write your program so that your report looks like this:

GRADE	MALE	FEMALE	TØTAL
A	35	50	85
B	35	40	75
C	20	20	40
D	30	30	60
F	15	15	30
TØTAL	135	155	290

Answers to Self-Test

The frame numbers in parentheses refer to the frames in the chapter where the topic is discussed. You may wish to refer back to these for quick review.

1. (b), (d), (e), and (f) are legal double-subscripted variables. (frames 5 and 6)

2. 3,2 meaning 3 rows, 2 columns. (frames 2, 3, and 4)

3. 100 DIM A(3,2) (frame 12)

4. A(3,2) (frames 9, 10, and 11)

5. (a) 1   (b) 5   (frame 11)

6. (a) 6   (b) 3   (frame 11)

7. 4   (frame 11)

8. Here is our program.   (frame 12)

```
10    DIM M[10,10]
20    FØR R=1 TØ 10
30    FØR C=1 TØ 10
40    M[R,C]=0
50    NEXT C
60    NEXT R
99    END
```

9. Remember the DIM statement.   (frames 16, 17, and 18)

```
10    DIM M[10,10]
20    MAT M=ZER
99    END
```

10. (frames 25 and 26)

```
10    DIM C[4,4]
20    MAT   READ C
30    MAT   PRINT C;
40    DATA 1,1,1,1,1,1,1,1,1,1,1,1,1,1,1,1
99    END
```

11. (frames 28 and 29)

```
10   DIM C[4,4]
20   MAT   INPUT C
30   MAT   PRINT C;
99   END
```

CHAPTER EIGHT
Subroutines

We're about to enter the realm of programs within programs, called *subroutines.* Subroutines provide an excellent method for organizing computer programs and help make programs easier to understand by breaking them down into functional parts — parts that may be reused in other programs as appropriate.

The format of this chapter is a bit different. If you know some statistics you'll have an opportunity to practice programming in that field; otherwise, you can by-pass the programming of statistical concepts and deal just with organizing programs with subroutines, which is the main concept of this chapter.

When you finish this chapter, you will be able to design programs in subroutine format, write appropriate main programs to access subroutines, and be able to use the following BASIC statements:

    GOSUB
    RETURN
    STOP

1. We've shown two computer program building processes. The first method was analogous to remodeling: the modification of an existing program. The second was building a program from the ground up. Now let us try building with prefabricated parts. This technique is handy for organizing a program according to the function performed by a group of one or more statements such as the sections of some programs you have seen earlier.

The prefabricated sections, or groups of statements, are called *subroutines.* The statement that tells a computer to go to a subroutine is, appropriately enough, the GOSUB statement. Like the GO TO statement, it is followed by a line number that corresponds to the first statement in the subroutine.

20 GOSUB 100   means skip to the subroutine in this program that has 100 as the line number of its first statement

The last statement in a subroutine is the RETURN statement. It automatically causes the computer to RETURN to the main program, i.e., to the line number immediately following the GOSUB statement that originally "called up" the subroutine. For example:

130 RETURN

This demonstration program shows how GOSUB and RETURN statements work.

```
5 REMARK HØW THE GØSUB STATEMENT WØRKS
10 REMARK MAIN PRØGRAM
20 GØSUB 100
30 GØSUB 200
40 GØSUB 300
50 PRINT "THIS IS THE END ØF THE MAIN PRØGRAM."
60 STØP

100 REMARK SUBRØUTINE #1 STARTS HERE
110 PRINT "THIS IS SUBRØUTINE #1 (OR 100)."
120 PRINT
130 RETURN

200 REMARK SUBRØUTINE #2 STARTS HERE
210 PRINT "THIS LINE CØURTESY ØF SUBRØUTINE #2 (ØR 200)."
220 PRINT
230 RETURN

300 REMARK SUBRØUTINE #3 STARTS HERE
310 PRINT "SUBRØUTINE #3 (ØR 300 IF YØU PREFER) AT YØUR SERVICE."
320 PRINT
330 RETURN

999 END

RUN

THIS IS SUBRØUTINE #1 (OR 100).

THIS LINE CØURTESY ØF SUBRØUTINE #2 (ØR 200).

SUBRØUTINE #3 (ØR 300 IF YØU PREFER) AT YØUR SERVICE.

THIS IS THE END ØF THE MAIN PRØGRAM.
```

Another helpful little statement often used in conjunction with GOSUB and RETURN is STOP. STOP has been used at the end of the GOSUB section of this program (Line 60). If it were not there, the computer would continue on down the program in line number order and once again process the subroutines, line by line, just as they appear in the program. To stop that from happening, a STOP statement is used. It acts like an END statement (but doesn't replace it). END must appear as the last line of all programs, and *cannot be used anywhere else.* STOP may be used whenever needed in a program, and, as a general rule, should appear at the end of the *main program*, before the subroutines start. In effect, the STOP statement tells the computer "GO TO END" (on some systems), or "END HERE."

Now examine the program, line by line, and see how it causes the output of the RUN. As an aid and an exercise, use the following blanks to show the actual order in which the statements in the program are processed. Place line numbers in each blank in the order that the computer will process the program.

————————   ————————

————————   ————————

————————   ————————

————————   ————————

————————   ————————

————————   ————————

————————   ————————

————————   ————————

————————   ————————

————————————————————————————————

5	220
10	230
20	40
100	300
110	310
120	320
130	330
30	50
200	60
210	999 (or not, depending on your system)

2.   We have modified a portion of the *main program* only of the program in frame 1. Notice how it changes the printout of the RUN.

```
20  GØSUB 300
30  GØSUB 100
40  GØSUB 200

RUN


SUBRØUTINE #3 (ØR 300 IF YØU PREFER) AT YØUR SERVICE.

THIS IS SUBRØUTINE #1 (OR 100).

THIS LINE CØURTESY ØF SUBRØUTINE #2 (ØR 200).

THIS IS THE END ØF THE MAIN PRØGRAM.
```

Here is another modification of the main program. What will the computer type when the program is RUN?

```
5   REMARK HØW THE GØSUB STATEMENT WØRKS
10   REMARK MAIN PRØGRAM
20   GØSUB 100
50   PRINT "THIS IS THE END ØF THE MAIN PRØGRAM."
60   STØP

RUN
```

———————————————————————————

```
RUN


THIS IS SUBRØUTINE #1 (OR 100).

THIS IS THE END ØF THE MAIN PRØGRAM.
```

3. Now try this one. What will the computer print when the program is RUN?

```
5    REMARK HØW THE GØSUB STATEMENT WØRKS
10   REMARK MAIN PRØGRAM
20   GØSUB 100
30   GØSUB 100
40   GØSUB 100
50   PRINT "THIS IS THE END ØF THE MAIN PRØGRAM."
60   STØP

RUN
```

_____

```
RUN

THIS IS SUBRØUTINE #1 (OR 100).

THIS IS SUBRØUTINE #1 (OR 100).

THIS IS SUBRØUTINE #1 (OR 100).

THIS IS THE END ØF THE MAIN PRØGRAM.
```

4.   Obviously, each of the little subroutines in our example could be changed or expanded to perform specific duties other than PRINT statements. In fact, each subroutine could be a complete program itself, to be accessed by a main program in any order that is convenient to the user and that also provides the results desired. Below is the TEST-SCORING PROGRAM which was developed in the last section of Chapter Six. (For a RUN, see Chapter Six, frame 44).

```
100 REMARK TEST SCØRING PRØGRAM
110 DIM C(100),A(100)

200 REMARK READ CØRRECT ANSWERS INTØ C(1) THRU C(N)
210 READ N
220 MAT READ C(N)

300 REMARK INPUT STUDENT'S ANSWERS, A(1) THRU A(N)
310 PRINT "YØUR ANSWERS";
320 MAT INPUT A(N)

400 REMARK CØMPUTE AND PRINT SCØRE
410 LET S=0
420 FØR Q=1 TØ N
430 IF A(Q)<>C(Q) THEN 450
440 LET S=S+1
450 NEXT Q
460 PRINT "YØUR SCØRE IS";S
470 PRINT
480 GØ TØ 300

900 REMARK VALUE ØF N AND C(1) THRU C(N)
910 DATA 8
920 DATA 3,2,3,1,4,2,1,4
999 END
```

How many times is the section beginning at Line 200 processed when the program is RUN? _____

How many times are the sections beginning at Line 300 and 400 processed when the program is RUN? _____

----

    one time (or as many times as the user wants to supply INPUT data)
    as many times as the user want to supply INPUT data

5.   As an exercise in the use of GOSUB's, modify the program in frame 4 to subroutine format. The main program should include Line 110 DIM as its first statement. All subroutines should be "called up" by statements in the *main program only*. Show your modifications below.

```
110 DIM C(100),A(100)
```

```
120 GØSUB 200
130 GØSUB 300
140 GØSUB 400
150 GØ TØ 130
230 RETURN
330 RETURN
480 RETURN
```

480 RETURN   Substitutes for old Line 480, whose function is now performed by Line 150 in the main program

The next section of this chapter will take you through the process of assembling a program from subroutine blocks that can perform a variety of common statistical computations. Using subroutines, the program is conveniently organized according to functions performed; that is, each subroutine does a particular part of the statistical computations.

The statistical measures to be discussed are: mean, variance, and standard deviation.

If you are familiar with these statistical measures and wish to sharpen your programming skills, continue on in this section of text. Otherwise turn to page 256, frame 10.

In this section you will have the opportunity to develop the computational subroutines themselves. Perhaps more important, however, you will gain skill in using subroutines as prefabricated mini (or not so mini) programs by assembling previously written subroutine units into a complete program. (To learn or review statistics, we recommend Donald J. Koosis: STATISTICS, from this same series of Self-Teaching Guides published by John Wiley & Sons.)

6.   The statistical measure used in previous examples in this book is the *average* or *mean* of values or scores obtained through some method of measurement or observation. The mean (referred to in statistics as *one measure of central tendency* of the data) is calculated by adding all the values and dividing that sum by the total number of values. In common statistical notation, the formula for the mean is:

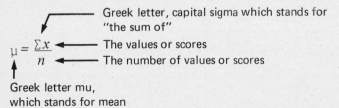

$$\mu = \frac{\Sigma x}{n}$$

Greek letter, capital sigma which stands for "the sum of"

The values or scores

The number of values or scores

Greek letter mu, which stands for mean

Each score in a set of scores lies some distance from the computed mean of the set; some scores may be just at the mean, some higher, some lower. The *variance* and its square root, the *standard deviation*, are measures of the "average" distance of all the scores in the set from the mean of the set. Statisticians call these "measures of variability (or dispersion)."

This is a computational formula for finding the variance of a set of scores or values:

$$\sigma^2 = \frac{\Sigma x^2}{n} - \mu^2$$

"The sum of"

The scores or values squared

The mean squared

Greek letter sigma squared, stands for variance

The standard deviation is the square root of the variance, and in statistical notation looks like this:

$$\sigma = \sqrt{\sigma^2} = \sqrt{\frac{\Sigma x^2}{n} - \mu^2}$$

We will use the following BASIC variables in the program:

N = n (the number of scores or values)
X = x (the scores or values)
M = μ (the mean)
T = Σx (the sum or total of scores)
D = Σx^2 (the sum or total of each score squared)
V = σ^2 (the variance)
S = σ (the standard deviation)

So let's get down to it. Write a subroutine to provide us with values for N, T, and D which are needed to calculate the mean and variance. The scores are provided in a DATA statement:

```
900   REMARK DATA FØLLØWS. DATA LIST ENDS WITH -1.
910   DATA 75,67,38,89,23,97,75,18,56,37,-1
```

Begin.

```
300   REMARK SUBRØUTINE: CØMPUTE N, SUM X, SUM X↑2
```

_____

```
300   REMARK SUBRØUTINE: CØMPUTE N, SUM X, SUM X↑2
310   LET N=0
320   LET T=0
330   LET D=0
340   READ X
350   IF X<0 THEN 399
360   LET T=T+X
370   LET D=D+X↑2
380   LET N=N+1
390   GØTØ 340
399   RETURN
```

7.   Circle the parts of the following formulas for which subroutine 300 calculates values.

$$\mu = \frac{\Sigma x}{n} \qquad\qquad \sigma^2 = \frac{\Sigma x^2}{n} - \mu^2$$

_____

$$\mu = \frac{\boxed{\Sigma x}}{\boxed{n}} \qquad\qquad \sigma^2 = \frac{\boxed{\Sigma x^2}}{\boxed{n}} - \mu^2$$

8.   Now write a subroutine to finish the computations for the statistical measures.

```
500   REMARK SUBRØUTINE: CØMPUTE MEAN, VARIANCE, STD. DEV.
```

```
500   REMARK SUBRØUTINE: CØMPUTE MEAN, VARIANCE, STD. DEV.
510   LET M=T/N
520   LET V=D/N-M↑2
530   LET S=SQR(V)
540   RETURN
```

9.   We want a RUN of the program to look like this:

```
RUN


N = 10
MEAN = 57.5
VARIANCE = 680.85
STANDARD DEVIATIØN = 26.0931
```

Complete the subroutine to print the results.

```
600   REMARK SUBRØUTINE: PRINT RESULTS
```

```
600   REMARK SUBRØUTINE: PRINT RESULTS
610   PRINT "N =";N
620   PRINT "MEAN =";M
630   PRINT "VARIANCE =";V
640   PRINT "STANDARD DEVIATIØN =";S
650   RETURN
```

10.   All you non-statisticians rejoin us here. We statisticians have written the following subroutines:

```
300    REMARK SUBRØUTINE: CØMPUTE N, SUM X, SUM X↑2
310    LET N=0
320    LET T=0
330    LET D=0
340    READ X
350    IF X<0 THEN 399
360    LET T=T+X
370    LET D=D+X↑2
380    LET N=N+1
390    GØTØ 340
399    RETURN
```

```
500    REMARK SUBRØUTINE: CØMPUTE MEAN, VARIANCE, STD. DEV.
510    LET M=T/N
520    LET V=D/N-M↑2
530    LET S=SQR(V)
540    RETURN
```

```
600    REMARK SUBRØUTINE: PRINT RESULTS
610    PRINT "N =";N
620    PRINT "MEAN =";M
630    PRINT "VARIANCE =";V
640    PRINT "STANDARD DEVIATIØN =";S
650    RETURN
```

```
900    REMARK DATA FØLLØWS. DATA LIST ENDS WITH -1.
910    DATA 75,67,38,89,23,97,75,18,56,37,-1
```

```
999 END
```

```
RUN
```

```
N = 10
MEAN = 57.5
VARIANCE = 680.85
STANDARD DEVIATIØN = 26.0931
```

Complete the main program so that the program will function as indicated in the preceding RUN.

```
100   REMARK MEAN, VARIANCE AND STANDARD DEVIATION
110   REMARK COMPUTE N, SUM OF X, SUM OF X↑2

120   _____

130   REMARK COMPUTE M, V, S

140   _____

150   REMARK PRINT RESULTS

160   _____

199   _____
```

- -

```
120   GOSUB 300
140   GOSUB 500
160   GOSUB 600
199   STOP
```

11. Now a nice thing about subroutines is that they may easily be changed or interchanged. (Non-statisticians can skip to frame 12.) Suppose that our data contained only two values or kinds of score. For example, we could score a voter poll using the value 1 to represent an "aye" vote and the value 2 to represent "nay" or "no opinion." The scores can then be tabulated or *grouped* by listing each kind of score (X) opposite its frequency (F), the number of times that that kind of score occurred in the data.

Suppose these are the data of two kinds:

1, 1, 2, 1, 1, 2, 1, 1, 1, 2, 1, 1, 1, 2, 2, 2, 1, 2, 2, 1

We can set up a table showing the "frequency of appearance" of each kind of data.

	X	F	
Kind of data (only two possible values)	1	12	} Grouped data (two groups or kinds)
	2	8	

So here are the data for the computer:

```
900   REMARK GRØUPED DATA FØLLØWS. DATA LIST ENDS WITH -1,-1.
910   DATA 1,12,2,8,-1,-1  ← There's the flag
```

There are 12 cases of value 1   There are 8 cases of value 2

The table below compares the formulas for mean, variance, and standard deviation for "ordinary" data versus grouped data.

STATISTIC	"ORDINARY"	GROUPED
mean	$\mu = \dfrac{\Sigma x}{n}$	$\mu = \dfrac{\Sigma(f \cdot x)}{n}$ where $(n = \Sigma f)$
variance	$\sigma^2 = \dfrac{\Sigma x^2}{n} - \mu^2$	$\sigma^2 = \dfrac{\Sigma(f \cdot x^2)}{n} - \mu^2$
S.D.	$\sigma = \sqrt{\sigma^2}$	$\sigma = \sqrt{\sigma^2}$

Translated into BASIC, we require values for 3 variables:

$T = \Sigma x$ or $\Sigma f \cdot x$

$D = \Sigma x^2$ or $\Sigma f \cdot x^2$

$N =$ the number of scores ($n = \Sigma f$ for grouped data)

In the DATA statement for grouped data, there are *pairs* of values: a score (X) followed by the frequency (F) of appearance of the score. There is also a double flag, which should be a programming clue for you that values are to be read in pairs. This is a sample DATA statement:

```
900   REMARK GRØUPED DATA FØLLØWS. DATA LIST ENDS WITH -1,-1.
910   DATA 1,12,2,8,-1,-1
```

With careful reference to the formulas presented, you should be able to complete the subroutine, particularly if you worked through the earlier statistics subroutines for ordinary (ungrouped) data.

```
400   REMARK SUBRØUTINE: CØMPUTE N, SUM X, SUM X↑2 (GRØUPED DATA)
```

```
400   REMARK SUBRØUTINE: CØMPUTE N, SUM X, SUM X↑2 (GRØUPED DATA)
410   LET N=0
420   LET T=0
430   LET D=0
440   READ X,F
450   IF X<0 THEN 499
460   LET T=T+F*X
470   LET D=D+F*X↑2
480   LET N=N+F
490   GØTØ 440
499   RETURN
```

12.   Non-statisticians rejoin us here. Look at subroutine 400 in frame 11.
For which BASIC variables are values computed? _____

   T, D, N   (any order)

13.   Look at subroutine 500 below, from our program in frame 10.

```
500   REMARK SUBROUTINE: COMPUTE MEAN, VARIANCE, STD. DEV.
510   LET M=T/N
520   LET V=D/N-M↑2
530   LET S=SQR(V)
540   RETURN
```

What variables must have values computed previously in order for subroutine
500 to compute M, V and S? _____

   T, D, N   (any order)

14.   Got the idea? Subroutine 400 for grouped data computes values for
the same variables that subroutine 300 (frame 10) computes "ordinary"
(ungrouped) data. Therefore, merely by substituting subroutine 400 for
subroutine 300 in the program you have a complete program for computing
the statistics for grouped data.
   If the DATA statement for grouped data is provided, show what modification of the main program (frame 10) is needed to RUN the complete
program for grouped data.

_____

   Change one line in the main program: **120   GOSUB 400**

SELF-TEST

This problem is intended to encourage you to examine any programming you do to determine whether subroutines will help make your program more efficient. It also provides an *algorithm* (algorithm? Well, a recipe is an algorithm. An algorithm is a well-defined procedure, or process, or step-by-step method for solving some kind of problem) that may be useful if you need to create programs to perform various clerical and filing tasks, or to sort any kind of numerical data.

1. Start with a list of numbers.

    3, 8, 3, 7, 8, 2, 9, 7, 3, 2, 6, 4

Sort them (arrange them) in *increasing* order:

    2, 2, 3, 3, 3, 4, 6, 7, 7, 8, 8, 9

We want a computer to do it for us. In fact, we'll also have the computer make up the original list of numbers, like this:

```
RUN

HOW MANY NUMBERS IN THE LIST TO BE SORTED?8
UNSORTED RANDOM NUMBERS: 85     51      27      67      12      87      98      72

NUMBERS AFTER SORTING: 12     27     51     67     72     85     87     98


HOW MANY NUMBERS IN THE LIST TO BE SORTED?2
UNSORTED RANDOM NUMBERS: 26     79

NUMBERS AFTER SORTING: 26     79


HOW MANY NUMBERS IN THE LIST TO BE SORTED?50
UNSORTED RANDOM NUMBERS: 18     98     22     96     22     5      7      15
 15     83     13     91     69     40     66     57     22     56     74     87
 23     50     63     28     62     62     17     30     39     83     53     83
 98     29     90     89     97     19     36     81     25     13     63     15
 36     6      81     41     34     17

NUMBERS AFTER SORTING: 5      6      7      13     13     15     15     15
 17     17     18     19     22     22     22     23     25     28     29     30
 34     36     36     39     40     41     50     53     56     57     62     62
 63     63     66     69     74     81     81     83     83     83     87     89
 90     91     96     97     98     98


HOW MANY NUMBERS IN THE LIST TO BE SORTED?51

SUBSCRIPT ERROR IN LINE 320
```

(a) If you would like to meet a real programming challenge, then try your hand at creating these subroutines. Otherwise, continue right on to reach part (b) and take a look at the subroutines in the Answers to Self-Test.

Subroutine 300 should generate a list of N random numbers from 0 to 99 stored by subscripted variable X.

Subroutine 400 should print the list of numbers stored by subscripted variable X.

Subroutine 500 should sort the numbers from smallest to largest.

(Programming hints: Use two FOR-NEXT loops, and a temporary storage variable to switch numbers from one subscripted variable location to another if the value of a variable with a smaller subscript is greater than the value of a variable with a larger subscript.)

(b) Now, look carefully at the RUN; then complete the main program. Our version of the main program contains 12 statements in addition to the REMARK statement.

```
100   REMARK NUMBER SORTING PROGRAM
110   _____
120   _____
130   _____
140   _____
150   _____
160   _____
170   _____
180   _____
190   _____
200   _____
210   _____
220   _____
```

BONUS PROBLEM. Look back to Problem 4 in the Self-test on page 165.
Write a new solution to this problem using subroutines. (You may want to
modify the solution on page 167 but you will probably find it easier to
rewrite the entire program.

Answers to Self-Test

The frame numbers in parentheses refer to the frames in the chapter where
the topic is discussed. You may wish to refer back to these for quick review.

1.   (frames 1, 4, and 15)

    (a)   Here are the subroutines:

```
300   REMARK SUBROUTINE: GENERATE NUMBERS X(1) THRU X(N)
310   FOR K=1 TO N
320   LET X[K]=INT(100*RND(0))
330   NEXT K
340   RETURN
400   REMARK SUBROUTINE: PRINT NUMBERS X(1) THRU X(N)
410   FOR K=1 TO N
420   PRINT X[K];
430   NEXT K
440   PRINT
450   PRINT
460   RETURN
```

```
500    REMARK SUBROUTINE: SORT NUMBERS - ASCENDING ORDER
510    FOR K=1 TO N-1
520    FOR J=K+1 TO N
530    IF X[K] <= X[J] THEN 570
540    LET T=X[K]
550    LET X[K]=X[J]
560    LET X[J]=T
570    NEXT J
580    NEXT K
590    RETURN
999    END
```

(b)
```
100    REMARK NUMBER SORTING PROGRAM
110    DIM X[50]
120    PRINT "HOW MANY NUMBERS IN THE LIST TO BE SORTED";
130    INPUT N
140    GOSUB 300
150    PRINT "UNSORTED RANDOM NUMBERS:";
160    GOSUB 400
170    GOSUB 500
180    PRINT "NUMBERS AFTER SORTING:";
190    GOSUB 400
200    PRINT
210    PRINT
220    GO TO 120
```

CHAPTER NINE
String Variables

The BASIC instructions you have learned up until now will work on most any version of BASIC. The chapters that follow will teach you about the advanced BASIC instructions, *string variables* and *files*. Some computers do not have these capabilities. In those that do, the instructions vary, though each system uses a similar set of instructions. So, if you follow the instructions for using string variables and files taught in these chapters, you may encounter some difficulty running the examples on your particular computer. Nonetheless, by learning one method well, you will have an easier time learning the same processes for your computer system. We suggest that after you complete these chapters you read the reference materials for your computer system to identify possible differences while the material is fresh in your mind.

In this chapter you will learn about string variables, the instructions that permit you to use alphabetic information. Upon completion of this chapter you will be able to write programs using these statements with string variables.

DIM	INPUT	PRINT	READ
DATA	LET	IF-THEN	

1. So far, your use of alphanumeric (that's mixed alphabetic and numeric) phrases has been limited to the use of strings in PRINT statements like this one.

```
10 PRINT "THIS IS A STRING"
```

Now we can add a new feature to BASIC, a string variable.

```
10 LET T$="STRING FOR THE STRING VARIABLE T$"
          ↑
```
This is a string variable

You identify a string variable by using a letter (A – Z) followed by a dollar sign ($). String variables permit you to manipulate alphanumeric data with greater ease. String variable instructions include: DIM, LET, PRINT, INPUT, READ, DATA, IF-THEN.

On most computers, each string variable that will be longer than one character must be DIMensioned to indicate the *maximum* size of the string it may contain. (A space is counted as one character.)

```
"THE LENGTH OF THIS STRING IS 43 CHARACTERS"
```

"SAM 123" This is a 7 character string (an auto license plate)

Here are examples of how you DIM string variables.

```
10 DIM A$(5)  ◄───────── Defines the string variable A$ with a
                          maximum size of 5 characters
20 DIM B$(10),C$(20) ◄─ Defines two string variables: B$ with
                          10 characters, C$ with 20
```

You can DIM numeric arrays and string variables in the same statement.

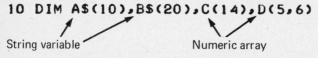

```
10 DIM A$(10),B$(20),C(14),D(5,6)
       ↗      ↗         ↖  ↗
String variable        Numeric array
```

The maximum possible size permitted for a string variable will vary from system to system. Refer to your system reference manual for the limits of your system. It may be as small as 6, though 72 is most common. A maximum of 255 characters is available on many newer computers.

```
10 DIM X$(14)
```

Up to how many characters are permitted in the string variable X$? _____

_____

14

2.   You can enter values of string variables in a program using an INPUT statement. First let's try a program with just one string variable to enter.

```
1    REM STRING NAME
5    DIM A$(15)
10   PRINT "WHAT IS YOUR NAME";
20   INPUT A$
30   PRINT "YOU SAY YOUR NAME IS";A$
99   END

RUN

WHAT IS YOUR NAME?HAROLD              Lines 10 and 20
YOU SAY YOUR NAME IS HAROLD           Line 30
```

Look what happened when we ran this same program again.

```
WHAT IS YOUR NAME?WEIRD HAROLD YOUNG    New string
                                       variable

BAD INPUT, RETYPE FROM ITEM 1
? WEIRD HAROLD          ? from our computer means INPUT again
YOU SAY YOUR NAME IS WEIRD HAROLD    It works this
                                     time
```

Look carefully at the program above. Why did the entering of the string variable WEIRD HAROLD YOUNG cause the computer to print the error

message? _____

_____

_____

The string variable A$ is only DIMensioned for 15 characters. WEIRD HAROLD YOUNG is 18 characters and therefore unacceptable.

3.   Modify the program in frame 2 to ask "WHAT IS YOUR STREET
ADDRESS?" and have the computer print name and address on two con-
secutive lines.

```
5   DIM A$[15],B$[20]
10    PRINT "WHAT IS YOUR NAME";
15    INPUT A$
20    PRINT "WHAT IS YOUR STREET ADDRESS";
30    INPUT B$
50    PRINT
60    PRINT "NAME: ",A$
70    PRINT "ADDRESS :",B$
99    END
RUN

WHAT IS YOUR NAME?HAROLD YOUNG
WHAT IS YOUR STREET ADDRESS?1327 WRIGHT STREET

NAME:          HAROLD YOUNG
ADDRESS :      1327 WRIGHT STREET
```

4.   On many systems if your INPUT statement asks for *more than* one string, you must enter each one enclosed in quotes and separated by a comma.

```
1   REM STRING DOUBLE INPUT
5   DIM A$[20],B$[20],C$[2]
10   PRINT "WHAT IS YOUR NAME";
20   INPUT A$
30   PRINT "WHAT IS YOUR CITY AND STATE";
40   INPUT B$,C$
50   PRINT
60   PRINT A$,B$,C$
99   END

RUN

WHAT IS YOUR NAME?GEORGE YOUNG
WHAT IS YOUR CITY AND STATE?"SAN FRANCISCO","CA"

GEORGE YOUNG    SAN FRANCISCO   CA
```

Show how you would enter the data requested in this question.

```
ENTER YOUR NAME AND SEX (M OR F)_____
```

_____

```
"GEORGE YOUNG", "M"
```

NOTE: For ease of operation, it might be wise to design your programs so that each string INPUT statement calls for only one value to be entered, thereby eliminating the use of quotes and a lot of confusion.

5.   Keeping in mind that you can only enter alphanumeric data using string variables, you are permitted to mix string variables and numeric variables in one INPUT statement, but the string variable must still be entered enclosed in quotes.

```
5    REM    STRING/VARIABLE INPUT
10   DIM A$[15]
15   PRINT "ENTER YOUR NAME AND AGE";
20   INPUT A$,B
25   PRINT
30   PRINT B,A$
99   END

RUN

ENTER YOUR NAME AND AGE?"GEORGE YOUNG",24

    24               GEORGE YOUNG
```

Show how George Young would respond to this question if he was born August 9, 1953.

```
ENTER YOUR YEAR OF BIRTH AND ASTROLOGICAL SIGN
```

_____

_____

1953, "LEO"

6.   Write a program to enter and print an auto license plate that has a 3 letter alphabetic string and a 3 digit number (i.e., SAM 123). Enter the letters as a string variable and the number as a numeric variable.

```
5   DIM A$[3]
10    INPUT A$,B
20    PRINT A$;B
99    END

RUN

?"SAM",123
SAM 123
```

Where did the space come from? BASIC reserves a place for the sign of the number (see next example)

```
RUN

?"MAX",-456
MAX-456
```

If you enter a negative number (which you normally wouldn't for this problem) it will look like this

7.   You can also enter string variables by using READ and DATA statements.

```
1   REM    STRING READ/DATA COURSE LIST
5   DIM A$[12]
10    PRINT "COURSE","HOURS","GRADE"
20    READ A$,B,C$
30    PRINT A$,B,C$
40    GOTO 20
50    DATA "ENGLISH 1A",3,"B","SOC 130",3,"A"
55    DATA "PHYSICS 2A",5,"C","STAT 10",3,"C"
60    DATA "BUS ADM  1A",4,"B","ECON 100",4,"B"
65    DATA "HUMANITIES",3,"A","HISTORY 17A",3,"B"
70    DATA "CALCULUS",4,"C"
99    END

RUN
```

COURSE	HOURS	GRADE
ENGLISH 1A	3	B
SOC 130	3	A
PHYSICS 2A	5	C
STAT 10	3	C
BUS ADM 1A	4	B
ECON 100	4	B
HUMANITIES	3	A
HISTORY 17A	3	B
CALCULUS	4	C

Examine DATA statements 50, 55, 60, and 65 in the program above. What is the difference in format between the string data in these DATA statements and the numeric data in DATA statements you have used before?

_____

_ _

When used in DATA statements, alphanumeric strings must be enclosed in quotes.

8. In the program in frame 7, why is there no DIM for C$? _____

_____

— — — — — — — — — — — — — — — — — — — —

C$ is not more than one character and therefore does not need to be dimensioned. (B is a numeric variable and therefore is not dimensioned.)

9. **3Ø PRINT A$,B,C$**

Look at the output produced by Line 30 in the program in frame 7. What is the function of the comma (,) in a string variable PRINT statement?

_____

_____

— — — — — — — — — — — — — — — — — — — —

Causes the output to be printed in up to five columns across the page (though here we only used three columns), just as with numeric variables.

Note. If the string variable size is greater than 15 characters, the PRINT column sequence will not be followed.

10. The string LET assigns a particular string to a string variable. Note that you must enclose the string in quotes as in these two examples.

```
10   DIM A$[12],B$[9]
20   LET A$=" GOOD EXAMPLE"
30   LET B$=" THIS IS A "

10   DIM A$(3),B$(2),C$(3)
20   LET A$="YES"
30   LET B$="NO"
40   LET C$=A$   ◄———————  C$ now contains "YES"
```

Write a string LET statement that assigns the course name Sociology to the variable S$.

_____

_____

— — — — — — — — — — — — — — — — —

```
5 DIM S$(10)
10 LET S$="SOCIOLOGY"
```

11.   The string IF-THEN allows you to compare *two* string variables.

```
10   DIM A$[3],B$[2]
15   LET B$="NØ"
20   PRINT "DØ YØU WANT INSTRUCTIØNS? YES ØR NØ";
30   INPUT A$
40   IF A$=B$ THEN 140
50   PRINT "THIS SIMULATIØN PERMITS YØU TØ REGULATE......"
     •
     •
     •
     •
     •
```

If you responded YES to the INPUT statement the comparison in Line 40 will be comparing the string variable A$ (YES) to the string variable B$ (NO). Because they are not equal the computer will execute the next statement, Line 50. If you responded NO, the program would jump to Line 140.

The comparison in Line 40 is between two _____ .

_____

string variables, A$ and B$

12.   You can compare a *string variable* to a *string*.

```
5   DIM A$[3]
10   PRINT "DØ YØU WANT INSTRUCTIØNS? YES ØR NØ";
20   INPUT A$
30   IF A$="NØ" THEN 140
40   PRINT "THIS SIMULATIØN PERMITS YØU TØ REGULATE ......"
     •
     •
     •
     •
     •
```

The comparison in Line 30 is between a _____ and a

_____ .

_____

string variable (A$)
string (NO)

You can't compare a numeric variable to a string variable.

IF A = B$ THEN 140 ← This is not permitted

13.   In a string IF-THEN, the comparison is made one character at a time. For example, if a space is introduced in the wrong place, it may cause a comparison other than what you expect.

```
10  INPUT A$

20  IF A$ = "MCGEE" THEN 140
```

If the user enters

```
?  MC GEE
```

the comparison will not be equal. Why will this comparison not be equal?

_____

_____

The space between C and G is a character which is not present in "MCGEE."

14. In addition to equal (=) comparisons, you can compare strings using the following:

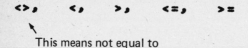

This means not equal to

It's a little tricky so you should use caution if you try them

The comparison is still made one character at a time from left to right. The *first* difference found determines the relationship. The relationship is based on position in the alphabet; C is "less than" S; T is "greater than" M.

```
10 LET A$="SMITH"
20 LET B$="SMYTH"
30 IF A$<B$ THEN 100
   .
   .
   .
```

In line 30 above, will the program branch to line 100 or continue to the next statement in sequence? _____

— —

Jump to line 100. The first difference is the third character and since I is "less than" Y, the IF THEN condition is true.

15. When you compare two strings of different length, the rule of first difference also applies. If the first difference is that one string ends before the other, then the shorter string is considered to be "less than" the longer one.

```
10 LET C$="SMALL"
20 IF C$<"SMALLER" THEN 140
30 LET D$="LARGEST"
40 IF D$>"LARGE" THEN 140
```

In the comparisons in line 20 and line 40 above, the program will jump to line 140 in both cases as the IF THEN condition is true in each case.

```
20 LET D$="COMPUTE"
30 LET E$="COMPUTER"
40 IF D$<E$ THEN 80
50 PRINT D$
```

What statement number will be executed next after the comparison in

line 40? _____

_____

line 80 as D$ (compute) is "less than" E$ (computer)

16. In frame 15, change Line 40 to read

```
40 IF E$> D$ THEN 80
```

Which statement will now be executed after the comparison? _____.

_____

Line 80. E$ is "greater than" D$.

17.   Before you proceed, we need to introduce the RESTORE statement and its use in connection with READ and DATA. A READ statement causes the *next* item(s) of data to be read from the DATA statements. If you want to start reading from the *beginning* of the data again, use a RESTORE statement which causes the next READ to begin at the first item of data in the first DATA statement.

   Now that you have seen how to use string variable comparisons, you can understand this simple information retrieval program that permits retrieving information from DATA statements.

   The program in frame 7, prints courses, hours, and grades. The program below permits the operator to enter the course; the computer will then print the course, hour, and grade.

```
10    REMARK STRING COURSE INFO RETRIEVAL
20    DIM AS[12],D$[12]
30    PRINT "ENTER COURSE NAME ";
40    INPUT D$
50    READ A$,B,C$
60    IF A$=D$ THEN 80
70    GOTO 50
80    PRINT A$,B,C$
90    RESTORE
100   PRINT
110   GOTO 30
120   DATA "ENGLISH 1A",3,"B","SOC 130",3,"A"
130   DATA "PHYSICS 2A",5,"C","STAT 10",3,"C"
140   DATA "BUS ADM 1A",4,"B","ECON 100",4,"B"
150   DATA "HUMANITIES",3,"A","HISTORY 17A",3,"B"
160   DATA "CALCULUS",4,"C"
170   END

RUN

ENTER COURSE NAME?ECON 100
ECON 100         4              B

ENTER COURSE NAME?HISTORY 17A
HISTORY 17A      3              B

ENTER COURSE NAME?ECON 2

OUT OF DATA IN LINE 50
```

Whoops, no such course. The computer read through all the data and found no such course; therefore, it printed this error message

Let's look at another RUN of the program.

RUN

ENTER COURSE NAME? SOC 130

OUT OF DATA IN LINE 50

Why did we get the error message this time? _____

_ _

The course name is stored SOC 130, but the user typed SOC130 without a space between SOC and 130.

18. What is the purpose of Line 60? **IF A$=D$ THEN 80** _____

_____

_ _

To test whether or not the course READ from the DATA statement is the course requested in the INPUT statement.

19. Which DATA items will be read when executing the READ statement in Line 50 after execution of RESTORE in Line 90?

_____

_ _

English 1A, 3, B, the first data items.

20. Modify the program in frame 17 so it will print the message "NO SUCH COURSE" instead of the data error message if the course you entered does not exist on the files. (You might try putting a "flag" at the end of the regular data as we did earlier in this book.)

_ _

```
55 IF A$="END" THEN 115
115 PRINT "NO SUCH COURSE"
118 GØ TØ 30
165 DATA "END",0,"0"
```

21. Using the data from the program in frame 17, write a program that will print a list of courses for which B grades were received.

```
1    REM STRING B LISTING
5    DIM A$[12]
10   READ A$,B,C$
20   IF C$="B" THEN 30
25   GØTØ 10
30   PRINT A$,B,C$
40   GØTØ 10
50   DATA "ENGLISH 1A",3,"B","SØC 130",3,"A"
55   DATA "PHYSICS 2A",5,"C","STAT 10",3,"C"
60   DATA "BUS ADM  1A",4,"B","ECØN 100",4,"B"
65   DATA "HUMANITIES",3,"A","HISTØRY 17A",3,"B"
70   DATA "CALCULUS",4,"C"
99   END

RUN

ENGLISH 1A      3           B
BUS ADM  1A     4           B
ECØN 100        4           B
HISTØRY 17A     3           B

ØUT ØF DATA   IN LINE 10
```

22. Modify your program in frame 21 by adding one line so that the program lists courses with grades of A *or* B.

```
22 IF C$="A" THEN 30

RUN

ENGLISH 1A        3              B
SOC 130           3              A
BUS ADM   1A      4              B
ECON 100          4              B
HUMANITIES        3              A
HISTORY 17A       3              B

OUT OF DATA   IN LINE 10
```

23. Now we're getting down to some nitty gritty rules that are only used once in awhile. Read through these so you will know they exist but don't memorize them. Look 'em up next time you need 'em.

A substring is a part of a string and is defined by using subscripts after the string variable, A$(10) or A$(1,5).

```
5 DIM A$(30)
10 LET A$="MY HUMAN UNDERSTANDS ME"
20 PRINT A$(10)  ← The substring begins at the 10th character
99 END              and includes all the characters that follow

RUN

UNDERSTANDS ME
```

Replace Line 20 with PRINT A$(15). What will be printed when the new Line 20 is RUN? _____

```
STANDS ME
```

24. Now look at these examples. To isolate one character you need to use the value twice indicating the first and the last character of the substring.

```
5    DIM A$[30]
10   LET A$="MY HUMAN UNDERSTANDS ME"
20   PRINT A$[4,4] ◄────── Will print H, the 4th character in the string.
99   END                  (A space counts as one character)
RUN

H
```

Here we have a substring that starts at character 1 and includes all of the characters through and including the 9th character.

```
5    DIM A$[30]
10   LET A$="MY HUMAN UNDERSTANDS ME"
20   PRINT A$[1,9]
99   END
RUN

MY HUMAN
```

In the program directly above, change Line 20 to read PRINT A$(4,8). What will be printed when the new Line 20 is executed? _____

_____

```
HUMAN
```

25. What will be printed by the following program?

```
10 DIM A$(20)
20 LET A$="GAMES COMPUTERS PLAY"
30 PRINT A$(7,15),A$(17),A$(1,5)
99 END
```

_____

```
RUN

COMPUTERS      PLAY           GAMES
```

26. Here are parts of a program to print the string variable A$ backwards, one character at a time. Fill in the blanks and show the RUN.

```
5   DIM A$(___)

10  LET A$="ABCDEFGHIJKLMNØPQRSTUVWXYZ"

20  FØR X=___TØ____ STEP -1

30  PRINT A$(X,___);

40  _____

99  END
```

_____

```
5    DIM A$[26]
10   LET A$="ABCDEFGHIJKLMNØPQRSTUVWXYZ"
20   FØR X=26 TØ 1 STEP -1
30   PRINT A$[X,X];
40   NEXT X
99   END

RUN

ZYXWVUTSRQPØNMLKJIHGFEDCBA
```

SELF-TEST

1.   Write a program to permit INPUT of a 5 letter word and then print the word backwards.

2.   Read a series of 4 letter words from DATA statements. Print only those words that begin with the letter A. Write the program.

3.   Modify the program of exercise 2 to print the words that begin with either the letter A or B.

4.   Again, modify the program in exercise 2 to print only words that begin with A and end with S.

5.   Some years ago, the auto industry was hard-pressed to come up with names for new cars. They used a computer to generate a series of 5 letter words. Write a program to generate 100, 5 letter words with randomly selected consonants in the first and third and fifth places and randomly selected vowels in the second and fourth places. (You might want to refresh your memory on the use of random numbers by reviewing Chapter Five.)

BONUS PROBLEM. You have the following DATA statements containing names in last-name-first order. Write a program to print these names first-name-first without the comma.

```
9000  DATA  "BUTLER,LINDA","ØLIVER,RACHELLE"
9010  DATA  "DANIELS,JAMES","JOHNSON,DIANE"
9020  DATA  "CASH,BETTY","BROWN,JERALD"
9030  DATA  "SMITHEY,BØB","ARLINE,KATHY"
```

Answers to Self-Test

The frame numbers in parentheses refer to the frames in the chapter where the topic is discussed. You may wish to refer back to these for quick review.

1. (frame 26)

```
10  REMARK STRING SELF TEST 9-1
20  DIM A$[5]
30  INPUT A$
40  FØR X=5 TØ 1 STEP -1
50  PRINT A$[X,X];
60  NEXT X
65  PRINT
70  GØTØ 30
99  END
```

2.   (frames 7, 11, and 24)

```
1    REMARK STRING SELF TEST 9-2
20   DIM A$[4]
30   READ A$
40   IF A$[1,1] <> "A" THEN 30
50   PRINT A$
60   G0T0 30
65   DATA "ANTS","GNAT","L0VE","BALD"
70   DATA "APES","BAKE","MIKE","KARL"
75   DATA "BARD","ALAS"
99   END
```

3.   Modifications only. (frames 7, 11, and 24)

```
40  IF A$(1,1)="A" THEN 50
45  IF A$(1,1)<>"B" THEN 30
```

4.   Modifications only. (frames 7, 11, and 24)

```
45  IF A$(4,4) <> "S" THEN 30
```

5.   (Chapter Five, frames 24 and 25, and Chapter Nine)

```
1    REM- STRING SELF TEST 9-5
5    DIM A$[5],B$[21]
15   LET A$="AEI0U"
20   LET B$="BCDFGHJKLMNPQRSTVWXYZ"
25   F0R X=1 T0 100
30   F0R Z=1 T0 2
40   LET B=INT(21*RND(0)+1)
50   PRINT B$[B,B];
60   LET A=INT(5*RND(0)+1)
70   PRINT A$[A,A];
75   NEXT Z
80   LET B=INT(21*RND(0)+1)
90   PRINT B$[B,B],
95   NEXT X
99   END
```

RUN

Z0KUC	BITUR	S0DUG	K0ZEM	PATAR
TIMUQ	S0ZIC	BAGUY	FIRIF	FULAD
FIZUX	NULUZ	DEXUJ	T0BIC	P0XAZ
ST0P				

(This is our RUN. Yours will be different.)

CHAPTER TEN

Files

The use of BASIC files is an advanced concept you may not find useful right away. *How* and *when* to use files is difficult to learn for the novice and you may find this chapter takes two or three readings to be fully understood. We suggest that you read this chapter once now to get a general idea of what files are all about. Then after you do some more BASIC programming and are comfortable with computers, come back and work carefully through this chapter.

When you have completed this chapter you will be able to:

- differentiate between serial and random access files.

- write data onto serial and random access files using FILE PRINT statements.

- read data from serial and random access files using FILE READ statements.

- use the following file commands with serial and random access files.

FILES   IF END   TYP

1.   Files are used to store numeric data and string variables for use at any time. Up to now you have had to enter your data using DATA statements as part of your program. Using files, you can enter and store large quantities of data using one program and then access the data at a later time using a *different* program. You can access the data or file with many different programs, something you have been unable to do before.

One way to look at the file is to imagine that it is a separate item from the BASIC program. Programs are used to read *from* or write *onto* the file. In an application that uses a file to hold all name and address information for the student body of a school, we might have a whole series of programs all using *one* file.

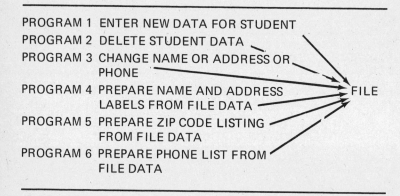

```
PROGRAM 1  ENTER NEW DATA FOR STUDENT
PROGRAM 2  DELETE STUDENT DATA
PROGRAM 3  CHANGE NAME OR ADDRESS OR
           PHONE
PROGRAM 4  PREPARE NAME AND ADDRESS        FILE
           LABELS FROM FILE DATA
PROGRAM 5  PREPARE ZIP CODE LISTING
           FROM FILE DATA
PROGRAM 6  PREPARE PHONE LIST FROM
           FILE DATA
```

One advantage of placing data into files instead of using DATA statements is

_____

_ _

You can access the data with more than one program.

2.   Later we will explain the use of serial files and random access files. This first section will deal only with serial files.

Information stored in a serial file can be viewed as a continuous series of data packed densely in the computer memory.

GEORGE/YOUNG/25/94191/BOB/HARRIS/42/83107/ . . .

To get to data in the middle of a serial file you must read from the beginning of the file, one piece of data at a time, until you reach the data you need.

Before you RUN a program using file commands you must *create* a file using the system command OPEN. Since OPEN is a system command it does not need a line number. Type,

OPEN — (name)

Hyphen   Rules for name vary with each system. Generally any name beginning with an alphabetic character and not exceeding 6 alphanumeric characters is acceptable. It is a good idea to use "reasonable" names so you can keep track of what they mean. A file of master student information might be called MASTER, a list of phone number PHONE.

What would you type to open the file that will contain student grades?

_____

- -

OPEN — GRADES (or any other name that makes sense to you)

3.   Which of the following file names will *not* be accepted by a computer that follows our general rules?

EYESORE   1ZERO   GRADEPOINT   A

3   PHONES   THREE

_____

- -

EYESORE (too big)
GRADEPOINT (too big)
1ZERO (begins with a number)
3 (begins with a number)

4. The amount of data (the number of pieces of data) that you can write onto the file will depend on the *size* of the file. The size of the file will vary from computer to computer. In some computers you determine the size of the file, in others, an opened file has a fixed size. (Consult your computer manual to find out how the file size is determined.)

File size is measured in units called *words*. Data written on a file uses up file words as follows.

Numeric variables— Each numeric variable uses 2 words of file space, whether the number has one digit or more.

String variables — Each character of a string variable takes approximately ½ word.

As an example, a file that will contain 100 names, each with as many as 20 letters or spaces will use:

String variable = 100 × 20 = 2000 characters
= 2000 × ½ = 1000 words of file space

A file that will contain 100 numbers will use:

100 × 2 = 200 words

Calculate how many words each of these sets of data will fill in a serial file.

(a)   140, 15-character names _____

(b)   140, 20-character addresses _____

(c)   140, 5-character zip codes (string variable) _____

(d)   420 numbers (representing responses to an opinion poll. Responses are 1, 2, or 3.) _____

(a)   140 × 15 × ½ = 1050
(b)   140 × 20 × ½ = 1400
(c)   140 × 5 × ½ = 350
(d)   420 × 2 = 840

5. At the beginning of a program that uses files you must include a statement which tells the computer which files are to be used by the program. The files statement looks like this:

```
10 FILES ABLE, C100, ZERØ
        ↖       ↑       ↗
        1       2       3
```

The order of the names in the FILES statement determines how they are referenced later in the program. The file named ZERO will now be referenced as file 3 in the program.

10 FILES ZERØ ,ABLE, C100

In this case, the file named ZERO will be referenced as file 1.

Write a FILES statement that will prepare the computer to use files named GRADES and MASTER.

_____

_____

10 FILES GRADES,MASTER

6.   A serial file READ statement permits reading data from an existing file. The general form is shown below:

READ # (file number) ; (variables)

Note the punctuation

For example:

20 READ #1;A

will read one piece of numeric data from the first file in the FILES statement and assign it to the variable A.

30 READ #3; A,B

will read two pieces of numeric data from the third file in the FILES statement and assign them to variables A and B.

Given the FILES statement, write a statement that will read three numeric variables from the file named ZERO.

10 FILES ABLE, C100, ZERØ

_____

_____

20 READ #3; A,B,C

7. You can also use a *calculated* value for the file number in a file READ statement.

20 READ #X; A\$,B

If in a previous statement, X has been calculated as equal to 2, the statement above will read from the second file in the FILES statement. The string variable (A\$) and the numeric variable (B) will be read each time Line 20 is executed.

Which file will be read in the following:

10 FILES PHØNE, MASTER, ZERØ
20 LET Y=3-1
30 READ #Y; A\$,B

_____

_____

MASTER

8 Files use a pointer ↑ that is always set to the NEXT piece of data to be read in the file. At the beginning of your program you should set the pointer to the beginning of the file. This file READ statement sets the pointer to the beginning of the first file in the FILES statement.

10 READ #1,1

Write a statement to set the pointer to the beginning of file C100 in this FILES statement.

10 FILES ABLE, C100,ZERØ

_____

_____

20 READ #2,1

9.   The pointer advances one piece of data (a complete string variable or one numeric variable) for each variable named in the file READ statement. (Remember, the pointer points to the *next* piece of data to be read.)

10 READ #1,1   Set the pointer to the beginning of the file

```
1     2     3     4     5    6    7     8    9     10
JOHN/JERRY/MARY/PETER/HAL/BOB/MIKE/MIMI/KARL/DAN
↑
```

**20 READ #1;A$**   Reads the first value, assigns it to A$ and advances
                          the pointer one data position to the second piece
                          of data in the file. (A$ = JOHN)

```
1     2     3     4     5    6    7     8    9     10
JOHN/JERRY/MARY/PETER/HAL/BOB/MIKE/MIMI/KARL/DAN
     ↑  (Now set to the second piece of data)
```

30 READ #1;B$,C$ Reads the next two pieces of data, assigns them
                       to B$ and C$ and advances the pointer to the 4th
                       piece of data which will be read next. (B$ = JERRY,
                       C$ = MARY)

```
1     2     3     4     5    6    7     8    9     10
JOHN/JERRY/MARY/PETER/HAL/BOB/MIKE/MIMI/KARL/DAN
               ↑
```

Indicate where the pointer will be positioned *after* execution of each of the file READ statements in this program.

```
1     REMARK FILE PØINTER
5     FILES DEMØ
10    READ #1,1
20    READ #1;A$
25    PRINT A$
30    READ #1;B$
40    READ #1;C$,D$
50    READ #1;E$
60    PRINT B$,C$,D$,E$
99    END
```

```
1     2     3     4     5    6    7     8    9     10
JØHN/JERRY/MARY/PETER/HAL/BØB/MIKE/MIMI/KARL/DAN
```

```
1     2     3     4     5    6    7     8    9     10
JØHN/JERRY/MARY/PETER/HAL/BØB/MIKE/MIMI/KARL/DAN
↑     ↑     ↑              ↑    ↑
10    20    30             40   50
```

10. A file we've called MASTER is in the format below, with name and address information for about 20 people.

NAME/ADDRESS/CITY/STATE/ZIP/PHONE NO/NAME/ADDRESS/CITY

Below is a simple program to read and print the contents of the file MASTER.

```
1     REMARK   MASTER FILE READ
10    DIM A$[15],B$[20],C$[10],D$[2],E$[5],F$[12]
15    FILES MASTER
20    READ #1,1  ← Sets the pointer to the beginning of the file
30    READ #1;A$,B$,C$,D$,E$,F$  ← Read from file 1. Each
40    PRINT                        time this statement is
50    PRINT A$                     executed, new values
60    PRINT B$                     are assigned to A$, B$,
70    PRINT C$,D$,E$               C$,D$,E$, and F$
80    PRINT F$
85    PRINT
90    GOTO 30  ← Go back to read more of the file
99    END
```

RUN

Below is the printout for the first two people from a RUN of the program above.

```
GEORGE YOUNG
1327 RIGHT STREET
BERKELEY            CA                    94107
405-321-1711


SANDY YOUNG
8 SHADY PLACE
OAKLAND            CA                    94203
405-122-1611
```

How many places does the pointer move each time Line 30 is executed?

_____

_____

6

11. What output (frame 10) would result if Line 90 read

90 GØ TØ 20

————————————————————————

The data printed for George Young would be repeated indefinately because Line 20 resets the pointer back to the beginning of the file. The rest of the file would not be read. This is a program error!

12. The program below prepares a list of names from the same MASTER file used in the preceding program.

```
1      REMARK MASTER FILE   NAMES
10     DIM A$[15],B$[20],C$[10],D$[2],E$[5],F$[12]
15     FILES MASTER
20     READ #1,1      Sets the pointer to the beginning of the file
30     READ #1;A$     Read the name
40     PRINT A$       Print the name
50     READ #1;B$,C$,D$,E$,F$
60     GØTØ 30
99     END

RUN

GEØRGE YØUNG
SANDY YØUNG
```

What is the purpose of Line 50? _____

————————————————————————

Moves the pointer forward 5 places to the next name.

13. Write a program that will print name and phone numbers from the file MASTER described in frame 10.

```
1     REMARK MASTER FILES NAME/PHONE
10    DIM A$[15],B$[20],C$[10],D$[2],E$[5],F$[12]
15    FILES MASTER
20    READ #1,1
30    READ #1;A$,B$,C$,D$,E$,F$
40    PRINT A$,F$
50    GOTO 30
99    END

RUN

GEORGE YOUNG          405-321-1711
SANDY YOUNG           405-122-1611
```

14. When the preceding programs are RUN, the computer prints an error message when the pointer detects that it has reached the end of the data. To avoid this error message, use the IF END statement, which causes the program to jump to another instruction when the end of the data is reached. IF END is also used to detect the physical end of the file. You may run out of data before reading to the physical end of the file and while loading a file you may reach the physical end of the file before all your data is entered. The IF END statement is used to avoid an error message in either of these cases. The general form of the IF END is shown below.

IF END # (file number) THEN (line number)

Once executed, the IF END statement does not have to be executed again
and again. It is like a 'flag'. Once "set", it stays "set" until the end of the
data is reached, or the end of the file is reached, or until a new IF END
statement is executed cancelling the earlier one. You should place the IF
END statement before the read statement in a file reading program.

Add an IF END statement to our file MASTER program below, that
will cause the program to jump to the end of the program when it reaches
the end of the data or the end of the file.

```
1     REMARK MASTER FILE  NAMES
10    DIM A$[15],B$[20],C$[10],D$[2],E$[5],F$[12]
15    FILES MASTER
20    READ #1,1

25    _____

30    READ #1;A$
40    PRINT A$
50    READ #1;B$,C$,D$,E$,F$
60    GOTO 30
99    END

RUN


GEORGE YOUNG
SANDY YOUNG


_____

25 IF END #1 THEN 99
```

15. The file PRINT statement is used to print data onto the file as opposed to printing data that is contained in the file. You use it to *load* your file with data. Here is the general form:

PRINT # (file number) ; (variables)

```
FILE #1    (EMPTY)

           5   READ #1,1
           10  PRINT #1;A,B,C$

FILE #1    A/B/C$/

           20  PRINT #1,D,E,F$

FILE #1    A/B/C$/D/E/F$
```

Set the pointer to the beginning of the file. Line 10 causes this information to be entered into the file. (A, B and C$ have already been assigned values elsewhere)

Line 20 causes D, E, and F$ to be printed onto the file immediately following the previous data (from the pointer)

A sample program sets up a small file of names and phone numbers from READ and DATA statements.

```
1    REMARK FILES PRINT
10   DIM A$[15],B$[12]
15   FILES PHONE
20   READ #1,1                Sets the pointer to the beginning of the file
22   IF  END #1 THEN 90       A safety check to avoid possible errors
25   READ A$,B$
30   IF A$="NO MORE DATA" THEN 99  TEST – Have we
40   PRINT #1;A$,B$           reached the end of the data? If not, print
45   GOTO 25                  what we have onto the file
50   DATA "GEORGE YOUNG","408-331-2234"
55   DATA "HAROLD JACKS","514-206-2056"
60   DATA "NO MORE DATA","DUMMY DATA "
90   PRINT "ERROR...END OF FILE"
99   END
```

If you RUN the preceding program nothing happens that you can see——it's all inside!——unless you hit the end of the file and Line 90 is executed.

(a)   Which statement tests for the end of file condition? _____

(b)   If the end of the file is encountered what will be printed? _____

(c)   Which statement causes the information to be printed into the file?

_____

_____

(a)   **22 IF END #1 THEN 90**
(b)   ERRØR...END ØF FILE
(c)   **40 PRINT #1;A\$,B\$**

16.   Fill in the missing blanks for the following program that READS the data from the MASTER file described earlier and creates a *second file*, PHONE, of names and phone numbers.

```
1    REMARK DØUBLE FILE USAGE
5    FILES MASTER,PHØNE
10   DIM A$(15),B$(20),C$(10),D$(2),E$(5),F$(12)
20   READ #1,1
25   IF END #1 THEN 99
30   IF END #2 THEN 90

35   READ #____;A$,B$,C$,D$,E$,F$

40   PRINT #____;A$,F$

50   GØTØ _____
90   PRINT "ERRØR...END ØF FILE 2"
99   END
```

_____

35 READ #1;   Read from file 1
40 PRINT #2;   Print onto file 2
50 GØ TØ 35   Go back for more data

17. Now let's combine some earlier problems with file capabilities. Write a program to load a file called RND with 200 random *integer* numbers from 1 to 4. (You might want to review the use of random numbers by rereading Chapter Five.)

```
1   REMARK RANDØM LØADER
5   FILES RND
7   READ #1,1
9   IF  END #1 THEN 90
10  FØR X=1 TØ 200
20  LET Y=INT(4*RND(0)+1)
30  PRINT #1;Y
40  NEXT X
45  GØTØ 99
90  PRINT "ERRØR....END ØF FILE"
99  END
```

18. Write a program that will read and print the 200 numbers in the RND file.

_____

Here are two possible solutions:

```
1    REMARK RANDØM READER
5    FILES RND
10   READ #1,1
15   IF   END #1 THEN 99
20   READ #1;A ← Notice we can assign
25   PRINT A;     this variable any
30   GØTØ 20      legitimate letter
99   END
```

```
1 REMARK RANDØM READER A
5 FILES RND
10 READ #1,1
15 IF END #1 THEN 99
20 FØR X=1 TØ 200
25 READ #1;A
30 PRINT A;
35 NEXT X
99 END
```

19. Write a program that will read the 200 numbers in RND file and print a frequency distribution indicating how many times each number (1 to 4) appeared in the file. This is very similar to the voter-analysis problems in Chapter Six and Chapter Seven. Here is a sample RUN.

VALUE	HOW MANY TIMES
1	60
2	30
3	50
4	60

```
1 REMARK RANDOM DISTRIBUTION
5 FILES RND
10 DIM A(4)
12 MAT A=ZER
15 READ #1,1
20 IF END #1 THEN 60
30 READ #1;Y
40 LET A(Y)=A(Y)+1
50 GO TO 30
60 PRINT "VALUE","HOW MANY TIMES"
80 FOR Y=1 TO 4
85 PRINT Y,A(Y)
90 NEXT Y
99 END
```

20. The TYP function detects the "type" of data that will be read next in the file. The TYP function looks at the data that the pointer is pointing at and indicates their type. It is used to avoid file read errors and to detect the end of the file. For example, if READ A$ is the next statement, but the pointer is at a number you will get a FILE READ error message, since A$ is looking for a string variable not a numeric variable. The TYP function may be used to avoid that kind of error. These TYPE rules apply to most computer systems:

TYPE 1 means next item is a number.
TYPE 2 means next item is a string variable.
TYPE 3 means end of file.

To test the type of data next in a file, we use the IF-TYPE statement. The general form of the IF TYP statement is

IF TYP (file number) = (type) THEN (line number)

```
10 IF TYP(1)=2 THEN 50
```
If the next data item in file 1 is a string variable, then go to Line 50

```
20 IF TYP(G)=1 THEN 80
```
If data in file G (numeric equivalent) is a number, go to Line 80

```
30 IF TYP(2)=3 THEN 99
```
If next data item in file 2 is end of file, then go to Line 99

Write a statement that tests to see if the next item of data in the file ZERO in the files statement is the end of the file. If so, go to Line 70.

```
10 FILES ABLE, C100, ZERO

20 _____
```

```
20 IF TYP(3)=3 THEN 70
```

21.   Here is an obvious use of the TYP function.

```
10 REMARK FILES TYP DEMØ
20 DIM A$[72]
30 FILES EXAM
40 READ #1,1
50 IF TYP(1)=1 THEN 80      Test to see if next item is a number
60 IF TYP(1)=2 THEN 110     Test to see if item is string variable
70 IF TYP(1)=3 THEN 140     Test to see if item is the end of file
80 READ #1;A
90 PRINT A;
100 GØTØ 50
110 READ #1;A$
120 PRINT A$
130 GØTØ 50
140 PRINT "END ØF DATA"
999 END
```

What does this program do? _____

_____

_____

Lines 50, 60, and 70 test the next data item in the file, determine the
type, and then cause that data item to be read and printed in Lines
80–90, 110-120, or 140, depending on the type. This process repeats
itself through the file to the end of the data. This program could be
used to read and print the contents of a file when you are not sure
what the file contains and you want to know (that happens sometimes!).

22. You may encounter some difficulties with serial files. Serial files are fine for data that do not change. If you want to add new data *past the last piece of data* simply read to the end of the data marker and then make your additions.

```
1 REMARK ADD TØ FILE DEMØ
10 FILES PHØNE
20 DIM A$(15),B$(12)
30 READ #1,1
35 IF END #1 THEN 70 ⎫  Read to end of data
40 READ #1;A$          ⎬
60 GØ TØ 40            ⎭
70 IF END #1 THEN 100 ◄─Test for end of file
75 PRINT"ENTER NAME"; ⎫
80 INPUT A$           ⎬  Enter new data
85 PRINT"ENTER PHØNE #";⎭
90 INPUT B$
95 PRINT #1;A$,B$
97 GØ TØ 75
100 PRINT"ERRØR... END ØF FILE"
110 END
```

Which statement caused the new data to be printed onto the file? _____

_____

```
95 PRINT#1;A$,B$
```

23. If you want to alter the contents in the *middle* of the file — watch out! Here's our file. We will demonstrate how to insert data or change data in the middle of this file.

NAME/PHONE/NAME/PHONE/NAME/PHONE/NAME

For this example, assume you have been notified that the second name in the file has a new phone number. If this were a file of 3×5 cards, you would simply pull the second card, change it and insert the card back into its previous position. However, this is a computer serial file. If you followed that logical procedure — read to the old number type in the new number and stop — the *remainder of the file will be lost!* That's the way serial files work!

To get out of this dilemma you have to "play games" with your computer. The easiest way is to create a new file that is used as a scratch pad; that is, a temporary place to store the information from the original file. Here is a step-by-step procedure.

(a) Read from the file copying it onto the scratch pad until you reach the data to be changed.
(b) Make your change and enter it on the scratch pad.
(c) Read the remainder of the file onto the scratch pad.
(d) When you reach the end of the file, read the corrected scratch pad back into the old file position.

Here is our program to change the phone numbers. This procedure may seem cumbersome but it will take very little computer time.

```
1    REM-FILES ALTER
5    DIM A$[20],B$[12],C$[12]
10   FILES PHONE,PAD
20   PRINT "ENTER OLD PHONE #";
30   INPUT C$
40   READ #1,1
42   READ #2,1
45   IF  END #1 THEN 200
50   READ #1;A$,B$
55   IF B$=C$ THEN 100
60   PRINT #2;A$,B$
70   GOTO 50
100  PRINT "ENTER NEW PHONE #";
105  INPUT B$
110  PRINT #2;A$,B$
120  IF  END #1 THEN 140
125  READ #1;A$,B$
130  PRINT #2;A$,B4
135  GOTO 125
140  READ #1,1
145  READ #2,1
150  IF  END #2 THEN 999
155  READ #2;A$,B$
160  PRINT #1;A$,B$
165  GO TO 155
200  PRINT "OLD NUMBER NOT IN FILE "
210  GOTO 20
999  END
```

C$ is the old number

Set the pointer to the beginning of both files

Read the old file.

Test the file phone number you are looking for

If the numbers do not match print old file onto PAD

Write the new data onto PAD. Lines 120 to 135 read remainder of the old file and print it onto the PAD

Reset pointers on both files

Lines 150 to 160 read PAD and print onto PHONE file

(a)   Which statement searches the file PHONE for the old phone number?

_____

(b)   Which statements transfer the data from PHONE to PAD? _____

_____

(c)   Which statement puts the name and new phone number in PAD?

_____

_____

(a)   50 READ $1;A$,B$
(b)   60 PRINT #2;A$,B$ and   130 PRINT $2;A$,B$
(c)   110 PRINT #2;A$,B$

24. If Line 200 is executed, what is it telling the operator? _____

_____

Old number is not part of the file.

25. Suppose one of your clients sends a note with his name and new phone
number and does not include his old phone number. Modify the program in
frame 23 so that the person's name (instead of the old phone number) is
entered and used to compare with the PHONE file. You can do it with just
4 changes.

```
1    REM-FILES ALTER
5    DIM A$[20],B$[12],C$[20]
10   FILES PHØNE,PAD
20   PRINT "ENTER NAME";
30   INPUT C$
40   READ #1,1
42   READ #2,1
45   IF  END #1 THEN 200
50   READ #1;A$,B$
55   IF A$=C$ THEN 100
60   PRINT #2;A$,B$
70   GØTØ 50
100  PRINT "ENTER NEW PHØNE #";
105  INPUT B$
110  PRINT #2;A$,B$
120  IF  END #1 THEN 140
125  READ #1;A$,B$
130  PRINT #2;A$,B$
135  GØTØ 125
140  READ #1,1
145  READ #2,1
150  IF  END #2 THEN 999
155  READ #2;A$,B$
160  PRINT #1;A$,B$
170  GØTØ 155
200  PRINT "NAME IS NØT IN FILE AS ENTERED"
210  GØTØ 20
999  END
```

As you can see, serial files are best used when you know in advance that you will not be making many changes in the file once it's set up. It's fine to READ from serial files but if you know you will have changes to make it might be best to start out by creating a *random access file*.

26.   A random access file is divided into a number of separate, discrete divisions called RECORDS. Each record has an assigned number. Each record may be viewed as a small serial file.

1	2	3	4	5

RANDOM ACCESS FILE

Records may be accessed *directly or randomly* without having to read through the entire file. Records may be changed easily without having to go through the procedure outlined for serial files.

The data in our previous example (the name and address file called MASTER) could be arranged in a RANDOM ACCESS FILE so that the information for each person would be assigned to a *separate* record.

1 NAME/ADDRESS/CITY/STATE/ZIP/PHONE/	2 NAME/ADDRESS/CITY ...

One advantage of random access files over serial files is _____

_____

_____

You can make changes in the data of a random access file without going through the cumbersome procedure necessary to change data in a serial file.

27. The random file instructions are very similar to serial file instructions. You use the same OPEN command and the same FILE statements. Here is the general form of random file READ

READ # (file number) , (record number) ; (variables)

This statement causes data to be read from a random access file (notice the use of comma and semicolon punctuation).

Here are some examples of random file READ statements.

10 FILES ZERØ,ABLE

20 READ #2,3;A$,B$ Will read A$, B$ from the file ABLE, 3rd record

30 READ #1,1;X,Y,Z   Reads X, Y, and Z from the 1st record in file ZERO

40 READ #2,1   Sets the pointer to the beginning of file ABLE (same format as that used with serial files)

More examples.

10 FILES C100,PHØNE
20 LET A=2
30 LET B=3
40 READ #A,B; D$,E$ Since A = 2 the statement says read
.   from the file PHONE, 3rd record
.   (B = 3)
.
.
50 READ #1,A; A$,B$

Which file number and record number will be read by Line 50? _____

_____

_____

File 1
Record 2

28. If this is your file, what data will be read by each of the READ statements below?

```
1                2                3                4                5
  JEAN/564-3231/NANCY/322-9038/MARY/311-6124/ANN/512-6014/DIANE/924-30786
```

```
10 FILES PHØNE
20 READ #1,3;A$,B$
30 READ #1,1; B$,C$
40 LET K=5
50 READ #1,K;A$,B$
```

- -

```
20 MARY, 311-6124
30 JEAN, 564-3231
50 DIANE, 924-3078
```

29. This program reads the MASTER file (now arranged as a RANDOM file with each person assigned to one record) and prints its contents.

```
1   REMARK-RANDØM FILE READ
10  DIM A$[15],B$[20],C$[10],D$[2],E$[5],F$[12]
15  FILES MASTER
18  LET K=1
20  READ #1,1      Set the pointer to the beginning of the file
25  IF  END #1 THEN 99
30  READ #1,K;A$,B$,C$,D$,E$,F$      K is the record number.
40  PRINT                           Watch what happens in
50  PRINT A$                        Line 88
60  PRINT B$
70  PRINT C$,D$,E$
80  PRINT F$
85  PRINT
88  LET K=K+1            Got that?
90  GØTØ 30
99  END
```

What statements were added or changed from the program in frame 10 to make this program use random files? _____

- -

Statements 18, 30, 88

30. Write a program that will print the name and record location number for each entry in file MASTER.

```
1    REMARK FILES NAME/LØCATIØN
10   DIM A$[15],B$[20],C$[10],D$[2],E$[5],F$[12]
15   FILES MASTER
18   LET K=1
20   READ #1,1
25   PRINT "NAME ","LØCATIØN"
30   IF  END #1 THEN 99
35   READ #1,K;A$,B$,C$,E$,F$
40   PRINT A$,K
45   LET K=K+1
50   GØTØ 25
99   END
```

31. The general form of random file PRINT is:

PRINT # (file number) , (record number) ; (data)

This statement prints data onto a random file. Here is an example:

```
10 PRINT #1,1;A$,B$      Print A$ and B$ onto record 1 of file 1

10 PRINT #A,B;A$,B$
```

In frame 30 you wrote a program to generate a list of names and the record location number of each set of data. Using this list you can make changes in someone's record.

First look up the name on the list and get the file *record location number.* Then, enter this information into this file and change or update the program.

```
1    REM-RANDØM FILE UPDATE
10   DIM A$[15],B$[20],C$[10],D$[2],E$[5],F$[12]
15   FILES MASTER
20   PRINT "ENTER RECØRD #";
25   INPUT K         Enter the record number of the party to be corrected
27   IF  END #1 THEN 99
30   READ #1,K    Set pointer to beginning of record to be changed
35   PRINT "ENTER NAME";
40   INPUT A$
45   PRINT "ENTER ADDRESS";
50   INPUT B$
55   PRINT "ENTER CITY"
60   INPUT C$
65   PRINT "ENTER STATE CØDE";
70   INPUT D$
75   PRINT "ENTER ZIP CØDE";
80   INPUT E$
85   PRINT "ENTER PHØNE #";
90   INPUT F$
92   PRINT #1,K;A$,B$,C$,D$,E$,F$
95   GØTØ 20
99   END
```

What does Line 92 do?_____

_____

Print the new data onto the file in record location K.

Use the following for quick reference.

To delete an entire record:

10 PRINT #1,5

This statement will place an end-of-record mark at the beginning of record number 5 thereby deleting any data in that particular record.

In random files, IF END works the same as with serial files.
IF END also detects end of record marks in random files.

The TYP function also works the same with random files. In addition to detecting numbers; strings, and end of file, TYP will detect an end of record using the number 4. The following statement tells the computer to go to Line 400 at the end of the record.

10 IF TYP(1)=4 THEN 400

SELF-TEST

You made it to THE END. This Self-Test reviews some of the problems you worked with in earlier chapters and applies these familiar concepts (says who?) to files.

1. Voter-analysis problems are a very common application of files. Refer back to page 191.

    (a)   Write a small program that will load the responses in the DATA statements (910 to 920) into a serial file called VOTES.

    (b)   Rewrite the main program so the data will be read from the file VOTE instead of DATA statements.

2.   Refer to page 272 of Chapter Nine. This course listing could, or should be placed in a file.

    (a)   Write a small program to load the data in Lines 50, 60, and 70 into a file called GRADES.

    (b)   Now write a program to print the contents of this file.

3.   Refer to page 278, Chapter Nine. Write an information-retrieval program to retrieve data from the file GRADES you prepared in question 2A above.

BONUS PROBLEM. Assume you have administered a 10-question multiple guess test, with 4 possible responses per question. The correct answers (1, 2, 3, or 4) are loaded into a file called KEY. Another file, ANSWER, contains a student number followed by the student's 10 responses for 90 students. Your task is to write a program that will print each student number and tell how many questions were responded to correctly.

Answers to Self-Test

The frame numbers in parentheses refer to the frames in the chapter where the topic is discussed. You may wish to refer back to these for quick review.

1. (a) (frame 15)

```
1    REMARK-FILES SELF TEST-10-1
5    FILES VØTE
10   READ #1,1
15   IF  END #1 THEN 930
20   READ V
25   IF V=-1 THEN 999
30   PRINT #1;V
40   GØTØ 20
910  DATA 1,1,2,2,2,1,1,1,2,2,2,1,1,1,2,1,2
920  DATA 2,2,1,1,1,2,1,2,2,2,1,1,2,1,1,2,1
925  DATA -1
930  PRINT "ERRØR...END ØF FILE"
999  END
```

(b)   (frames 10, 17)

```
1 REMARK -FILES SELF TEST 10-1B
5  FILES VØTE
10   DIM C[20]
20   MAT C=ZER
30   READ #1,1
40   READ #1;V
50   IF V=-1 THEN 80
60   LET C[V]=C[V]+1
70   GØTØ 40
80   FØR K=1 TØ 2
90   PRINT "ANSWER NØ.";K;":";C[K]
100   NEXT K
199   END
```

2.   (a)   (frame 15)

```
1   REMARK-FILES SELF TEST 10-2
5   FILES GRADES
10   DIM A$[12]
20   READ #1,1
30   IF  END #1 THEN 90
35   READ A$,B,C$
40   PRINT #1;A$,B,C$
45   GØTØ 35
50   DATA "ENGLISH 1A",3,"B","SØC 130",3,"A"
55   DATA "PHYSICS 2A",5,"C","STAT 10",3,"C"
60   DATA "BUS ADM 1A",4,"B","ECØN 100",4,"B"
65   DATA "HUMANITIES",3,"A","HISTØRY 17A",3,"B"
70   DATA "CALCULUS",4,"C"
90   PRINT "ERRØR...END ØF FILE"
99   END
```

(b)   (frames 10, 17)

```
1   REMARK FILES SELF TEST 10-2B
5   FILES GRADES
10   DIM A$[12]
15   IF  END #1 THEN 99
20   READ #1,1
25   READ #1;A$,B,C$
30   PRINT A$,B,C$
40   GØTØ 25
99   END
```

3.   (frames 23, 24, 25)

```
1    REMARK FILES SELF TEST 10-3
5    FILES GRADES
10   DIM AS[12],DS[12]
15   PRINT "ENTER COURSE NAME";
20   INPUT DS
25   READ #1,1
30   IF  END #1 THEN 90
40   READ #1;AS,B,CS
50   IF AS=DS THEN 70
60   GOTO 40
70   PRINT AS,B,CS
75   PRINT
80   GOTO 15
90   PRINT "COURSE NAME NOT IN FILE"
95   GOTO 15
99   END
```

Final Self-Test

1. Look at Chapter Two Self-Test, question 6. The program you wrote calculated the value of two possible prizes:

   PRIZE NO. 1: N dollars
   PRIZE NO. 2: D dollars, where $D = 1.01^N$

   Write a program (or modify the one we used) to find the *smallest* whole number N for which PRIZE NO. 2 is greater than PRIZE NO. 1. Only this number should be printed.

2. Write a program to simulate the game of "craps." In this game two dice are rolled, and the total of the two dice is observed. On the first roll (of 2 dice), 2, 3, and 12 are losers ("craps"); 7 and 11 are winners. If the first roll totals 4, 5, 6, 8, 9, or 10, the dice are rolled again until the total is repeated (which wins) or until a 7 is rolled (which loses). (Hint: use a subroutine to throw the two dice each time.)
   Here are two sample RUNs.

   ```
   ØN THE FIRST RØLL, THE DICE TØTALED 9
   RØLLED AGAIN.........DICE TØTALED  5
   RØLLED AGAIN.........DICE TØTALED  9
   ITS A WINNER!!!!  HERE WE GØ AGAIN!


   ØN THE FIRST RØLL, THE DICE TØTALED 3
   ITS A LØSER....LET'S TRY AGAIN.
   ```

3.   Now, try a problem with matrices. Write a program that will *transpose* a 2 × 3 matrix. When a matrix is transposed, the rows become columns, and the columns become rows. The transposed matrix will be 3 × 2. For example:

```
RUN


HERE  IS  THE  ØRIGINAL:
   1      2      3

   4      5      6


AND  HERE  IS  THE  TRANSPØSE:
   1      4

   2      5

   3      6
```

4.   Write a program that will convert any input number from centimeters to inches, and/or from inches to centimeters, depending on the wishes of the user. Answers should be rounded to two decimals. (Use DEF FN)

Conversion factors:

1 inch = 2.540 centimeters
1 cm = .39370 inch

Use a string IF to decide in which direction the conversion is to be made. Here is a sample RUN.

```
RUN


LENGTH?1
IS  THAT  IN  CENTIMETERS,  ØR  IN  INCHES? INCHES
  1     INCHES  EQUALS  2.54         CENTIMETERS.

LENGTH?100
IS  THAT  IN  CENTIMETERS,  ØR  IN  INCHES?CENTIMETERS
  100   CENTIMETERS  EQUALS  39.37        INCHES.

LENGTH?
DØNE
```

Answers

1.   Here is our shortest program.

```
10   FØR N=10 TØ 1000
20   IF 1.01↑N>N THEN 40
30   NEXT N
40   PRINT "THE SMALLEST N IS:";N
99   END
```

Here is the RUN

```
RUN


THE SMALLEST N IS: 652

DØNE
```

2.   Here is our program.

```
10   REMARK FINAL TEST QUESTIØN 2: GAME ØF CRAPS
20   GØSUB 260
30   LET C1=A+B
40   PRINT "ØN THE FIRST RØLL, THE DICE TØTALED";C1
50   IF C1=2 THEN 170
60   IF C1=3 THEN 170
70   IF C1=12 THEN 170
80   IF C1=7 THEN 210
90   IF C1=11 THEN 210
100  REMARK C1 IS NØW THE 'PØINT.'
110  GØSUB 260
120  LET C2=A+B
130  PRINT "RØLLED AGAIN.........DICE TØTALED ";C2
140  IF C2=C1 THEN 210
150  IF C2=7 THEN 170
160  GØTØ 110
170  PRINT "ITS A LØSER....LET'S TRY AGAIN."
180  PRINT
190  PRINT
200  GØTØ 20
210  PRINT "ITS A WINNER!!!!  HERE WE GØ AGAIN!"
220  PRINT
230  PRINT
240  GØTØ 20
260  REMARK A AND B ARE THE DICE.
270  LET A=INT(6*RND(0))+1
280  LET B=INT(6*RND(0))+1
290  RETURN
999  END
```

3.   Here is our answer.

```
10   REMARK FINAL TEST QUESTION 3: MATRIX TRANSPOSE
20   DIM A[2,3],B[3,2]
30   MAT  READ A
40   DATA 1,2,3,4,5,6
50   FOR I=1 TO 2
60   FOR J=1 TO 3
70   B[J,I]=A[I,J]
80   NEXT J
90   NEXT I
100  PRINT "HERE IS THE ORIGINAL:"
110  MAT  PRINT A;
120  PRINT
130  PRINT "AND HERE IS THE TRANSPOSE:"
140  MAT  PRINT B;
999  END
```

4.   Here is one solution. Note that the rounding is done in the same step as
      the conversion, using DEF FN.

```
1    REMARK FINAL TEST QUESTION 4: CONVERTER
10   DIM A$[12]
20   DEF FNC(X)=INT(254*X)/100
30   DEF FNI(X)=INT(39.37*X)/100
40   PRINT "LENGTH";
50   INPUT L
60   PRINT "IS THAT IN CENTIMETERS, OR IN INCHES";
70   INPUT A$
80   IF A$="CENTIMETERS" THEN 120
90   IF A$="INCHES" THEN 150
100  PRINT "TRY AGAIN...";
110  GOTO 60
120  PRINT L;"CENTIMETERS EQUALS";FNI(L);"INCHES."
130  PRINT
140  GOTO 40
150  PRINT L;"INCHES EQUALS";FNC(L);"CENTIMETERS."
160  PRINT
170  GOTO 40
999  END
```

References

Question	Chapter(s)
1	1–4
2	1–5
3	7
4	7–10

Index